# Sulcata and Leopard Tortoises

Complete Herp Care

Ali,

BEST WISHES...

E. J. Pirog

EJ Pirog

# Sulcata and Leopard Tortoises

Project Team
Editor: Thomas Mazorlig
Indexer: Lucie Haskins
Cover Design: Mary Ann Kahn
Design: Patti Escabi

T.F.H. Publications
President/CEO: Glen S. Axelrod
Executive Vice President: Mark E. Johnson
Publisher: Christopher T. Reggio
Production Manager: Kathy Bontz

T.F.H. Publications, Inc.
One TFH Plaza
Third and Union Avenues
Neptune City, NJ 07753

Printed and bound in China,
08 09 10 11 12   1 3 5 7 9 8 6 4 2

ISBN 978-0-7938-2898-2

Library of Congress Cataloging-in-Publication Data
Pirog, E. J. (Edward)
  Sulcata and leopard tortoises : complete herp care / E.J. Pirog.
      p. cm.
  Includes bibliographical references and index.
  ISBN 978-0-7938-2898-2 (alk. paper)
  1. African spurred tortoises as pets. 2. Leopard tortoises as pets. I. Title.
  SF459.T8P57 2008
  639.3'924—dc22
                                  2008018208

The Leader In Responsible Animal Care For Over 50 Years!®
www.tfh.com

# Table of Contents

The continent of Africa is home to a variety of tortoises that are commonly kept as pets. Two of the most popular African tortoises are also the largest tortoises found there. Those tortoises are the leopard tortoise (*Geochelone pardalis*) and the African spurred tortoise (*Geochelone sulcata*), or sulcata as it is affectionately called by many keepers of this species.

Both of these tortoises were not commonly kept until fairly recently. In fact, up until about 20 years ago the spurred tortoise was rare among tortoise keepers. Because of the sulcata's hardiness and its willingness to breed in captivity, it is now one of the most commonly kept tortoises in the hobby. On the other hand, the leopard tortoise has always been a popular tortoise among tortoise keepers because of its distinctive and very attractive leopard pattern. It is not quite as hardy and adaptable as the sulcata.

These two tortoises both make wonderful companions, but because of their potential size as adults they require special and very careful consideration before adding one or more of them to your family. As babies, they have the cute appearance of other little tortoises, but the prospective keeper must realize that they do not stay that cute little size for very long. This dramatic change in size is one of the most important aspects to consider before obtaining one of these fantastic tortoises.

This guide is intended to give the keeper a good general idea of care involved in maintaining these two wonderful species in captivity. It discusses their environmental and dietary requirements and provides information

about their breeding, but it is not intended to be all-inclusive.

It is important to note that there are many additional sources of information on tortoise care; there are a number of books, all the information available through clubs, and numerous tortoise care websites. It would sometimes seem that there are great contradictions in styles, information, and methods for keeping the tortoises. What should be understood from the start is that there is no one single best way to maintain these creatures in captivity. It quickly comes to light that there are many variables in husbandry that are dependent on one another. Changing one or more of those variables (e.g., temperature) can usually be compensated for or can lead to a change in another (e.g., humidity). It is for this reason that it is highly recommended that a keeper gather as much information as possible in the quest to properly care for a pet tortoise. The goal is to provide the best conditions possible for a particular animal. Along with the gathered information, it is also important to pay particular attention to the tortoise in your specific care and see how it responds to the captive conditions. It is the tortoise itself that is the best tell-tale indicator as to whether the conditions provided are acceptable or not.

Keeping leopard tortoises or sulcatas in captivity can sometimes present challenges, but those challenges can be minimized if careful thought and planning are exercised before the actual acquisition of the tortoise. Once this is considered and understood, the keeping of these tortoises can be a life-long and very rewarding experience.

# Chapter 1

# Natural History

**W**hen obtaining a new pet such as a tortoise, it is always a good idea to become familiar with the natural history of the animal. This will give you some insight into the tortoise's life and behavior and a general idea of the care it needs. Knowing something about its feeding habits, environmental conditions, and natural behaviors will be helpful in providing a healthy captive environment.

Both the leopard tortoise and the African spurred tortoise share very similar dietary needs and preferences, but they differ quite a bit in both their natural habits and behavior. Although the two tortoises' ranges come very close in the area of Ethiopia, there is only anecdotal evidence to suggest that they actually occur together.

## African Spurred Tortoise

The African spurred tortoise obtains its common name from the large spurs (which are formed from modified scales) situated on the back of each hind leg. The scientific name (*Geochelone sulcata*) of this tortoise is derived from the distinctive growth rings or grooves that are produced around the scutes with each growth cycle (*sulcus* meaning a "groove or furrow"). Tortoise keepers often refer to this species as the sulcata to avoid confusion with the spur-thighed tortoise (*Testudo graeca*), a very different species.

The African spurred tortoise can be described as round in shape, with the shell being patternless and more flat than it is domed. New shell growth is seen around each scute as a dark brown ring, and this becomes sun bleached to a straw color as the tortoise gets older. The most distinctive feature of this tortoise is the large spiky appearance of the scales on the forelimbs.

There is a sexual dimorphism in this species, but it does not become clear until the tortoise is at least 10 to 15 pounds (4.5 to 6.8 kg) in size. The male will develop a concave

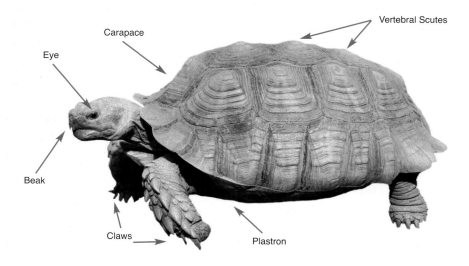

Carapace

Vertebral Scutes

Eye

Beak

Claws

Plastron

*Sulcata and Leopard Tortoises*

plastron, with the anal scutes forming a V where the tail protrudes. The male's tail will also be much longer than that found on the female. The tail on a male will wrap around to the back of the thigh. The female's body is usually more elongated in shape. The plastron will be flat, and the anal scutes will form a U shape where the tail protrudes. These characteristics become more pronounced as the tortoise gets bigger in size.

## Natural Range and Habitat

The natural range of the sulcata is roughly a 250-mile (402-km) wide strip of land that straddles the 15-degree north latitude—a line that is drawn from Senegal to the small country of Eritrea just north of Ethiopia. This relatively narrow strip of land that traverses the northern part of the African continent roughly corresponds with the transition zone between the Sahara Desert and the savannah and forests of the Sudan region to the south of the Sahara. This zone is sometimes referred to as the Sahel. It is a very specialized ecosystem that is characterized by short shrubs, grasses, and dwarfed trees for the most part. It is not quite desert and not quite savannah. It is important to note that because of its location, the Sahel can be more desert-like in some years and more savannah-like during other years, depending on the prevailing weather patterns. In a given year it can receive from 5 to 20 inches (12.7 to 50.8 cm) of rain, which is usually deposited during the monsoon season. The monsoon season is a relatively predictable season that can last up to 6 months. This rainy season usually occurs from July to November.

Another important point is that the Sahel is a transition zone between the desert and the Sudan region not only in weather but also in soil fertility. It is more fertile than the desert but less so than the Sudan region. This is important because even during times of good rainfall the vegetation is still stunted because of this infertile soil.

The sulcata digs extensive burrows in the soft soil during the monsoonal season. This provides a refuge from the extreme heat of the dry season in addition to the high midday temperatures that occur during the entire year. These burrows can extend well over 20 feet (6.1 m) in vertical depth, with a horizontal length of over 30 feet (9.1 m) in many cases.

## Spurred or Spur-Thighed?

*Geochelone sulcata* is commonly called the spurred tortoise. This sometimes causes confusion with the spur-thighed tortoise, which is one common name for *Testudo graeca*. It is for this reason that sulcata is gaining popularity as the common name for *Geochelone sulcata*.

The tunnels excavated by the tortoise can have multiple chambers and connecting tunnels where other animals (including snakes, lizards, birds, and rodents) sometimes seek refuge. On occasion these animals will die in the burrows. The animal carcasses will also serve as resources of food for the tortoise during hard times. Because of the depth of these burrows, the tortoise can find a relatively stable environment with steady temperatures despite the huge fluctuations outside the burrow. The humidity is also relatively high in the burrows, with levels of over 50 percent not being uncommon.

A sulcata's forelimbs have strong enlarged scales used to dig extensive burrows.

The activity level for the sulcata is relatively low during the height of the dry season, when they are seldom seen outside their burrows. With the approach of the rainy season, they will emerge to forage and replace lost water and nutrient reserves. It is during this time that most of the breeding and egg laying takes place, although there is not an exclusive breeding season. Because of low population densities males will usually breed throughout the year, mating with a female whenever one is encountered. This is most frequent when they are most active, which is during the beginning of the rainy season and towards the end.

## Natural Diet

The sulcata is an opportunistic feeder (as most tortoises are). During the rainy season it will feed mostly on the lush green growth that follows the plentiful rain. The menu includes grasses, broadleaf weeds, leaves, and fruit from trees and bushes. When the monsoon season passes, sulcatas will feed on almost any organic matter they can find and fit into their mouths, including the dried plants and leaves that remain during the dry season. They have been known to consume bark, small branches, animal feces, and carrion during times of little or no plant growth.

## Big Boys

The African spurred tortoise is the third largest tortoise in the world, superseded in size by only the Galapagos and the Aldabra tortoises (*Geochelone nigra* and *G. gigantea* respectively). The sulcata can attain a weight of over 200 lbs (90.7 kg). This is one of the most daunting attributes of this tortoise when considering one as a pet.

## Reproduction

Nestings in the wild have been reported to occur at the base of bushes and the like. Egg laying has been recorded from November to May, as many as 24 eggs being laid. There is a correlation between the number of eggs laid and the size of the eggs. In a single clutch, fewer eggs result in larger sizes and more eggs result in smaller eggs, assuming the females in question are of similar size. These eggs can take from 100 to close to 200 days to hatch, depending on the time of year the eggs were laid. Cooler temperatures result in longer incubation times.

Baby spurred tortoises are relatively large and quick on emergence from the nest. They grow at a relatively fast rate in the wild; there are reports of hatchlings attaining a weight of up to 2 pounds (1 kg) in the first year and weights up to 6.6 pounds (3 kg) after the second year. This depends on the time of hatching and the prevailing conditions of that time. Adult size can be reached in a relatively short time, but it will, again, depend on many factors.

## Leopard Tortoise

The leopard tortoise (*Geochelone pardalis*) gets its name from the leopard-like pattern that appears on the carapace. The base color is usually straw yellow with splashes of jet black distributed evenly over the shell. In the wild, adult leopard tortoises can obtain a size of over 110 pounds (50 kg) but are more typically in the range of 22 to 33 pounds (10 to 15 kg) as adults. They typically range from 15.75 to 20 inches (40 to 50 cm) in length.

The leopard tortoise has a fairly unique body shape. Its shell is usually relatively highly domed and the body more round in shape than long. It is interesting to note that the scutes on the carapace may be naturally pyramided (slightly raised in height somewhat

Leopard tortoise on the side of a dirt road in South Africa.

**The leopard tortoise is a distinctive tortoise that gets its common name from the spotted leopard-like pattern that adorns its shell. This tortoise has the most extensive range of all African tortoises, and the pattern varies greatly over that range.**

resembling a pyramid) on animals obtained out of the wild. This can be seen in roughly half the animals encountered. In most tortoises, pyramiding of the shell is seen mainly in captivity.

The two forms of the leopard tortoise used to be considered two different subspecies. They were called *Geochelone pardalis pardalis* and *Geochelone pardalis babcocki*. *Geochelone p. pardalis* is found in southern South Africa and southern Namibia. *Geochelone p. babcocki* is found from northern South Africa and Namibia east of the Great Rift Valley up to Ethiopia. The most distinguishing and most reliable difference between the two forms is the shell pattern of the juveniles. Juveniles of *Geochelone p. pardalis* are recognized by multiple spots on the center of each individual carapace scute. The pattern found on juvenile *Geochelone. p. babcocki* will vary from having no spots at all to having one spot and to having one spot attached to a scute border. A few other characteristics, such as size of adults and shell shape, have also been mentioned as differences, but they are too inconsistent to be used for any definite identification purposes, probably because of the overlapping range of the two forms. Currently the general consensus is to recognize only one species of leopard tortoise with no subspecies.

## Natural Range and Habitat

The leopard tortoise has an extensive range in both geography and topography. Those in the northern part of its range tend to follow the same activity pattern as the sulcata. The leopard tortoises found in the southern and central portion of the range tend to be active in the late spring to early fall. This would be about the months of September to February, considering that the range is in the southern hemisphere. In the far south to the central range, the leopard actually goes into a winter rest period that some would consider a form of hibernation. During this time, the tortoises will seek refuge in abandoned animal burrows or any other nook or cranny where they can escape the cold and remain dry. In the warmer part of its range during periods of extreme heat or drought, the leopard tortoise is known to estivate in similar fashion. Unlike the spurred tortoise, the leopard tortoise does not excavate its own burrow.

The leopard tortoise seems to be quite versatile in its selection of preferred habitat. It has been found from semi-desert to grasslands to scrublands to forest. Some have taken this information as evidence to support the idea that there may be more than one subspecies or species of leopard tortoise. There has been some speculation that the populations found in one habitat fail to do well in the habitat of other leopard tortoises. This could be a reason that some tortoises taken out of the wild fail to adapt to captivity; keepers often assume they all come from the same habitat or same general conditions, which is not the case.

## Natural Diet

Like most other tortoises, the leopard tortoise is an opportunistic feeder. In the wild it has been observed feeding mainly on grasses, various weeds, and the leaves of bushes and trees. It has also been observed consuming carrion and animal feces.

## Reproduction

In the wild the leopard tortoise breeds in the springtime, with egg deposition beginning in the late spring. Breeding and nesting can continue into the late fall. The female leopard tortoise can lay three or more clutches consisting of 5 to 20 (or sometimes more) eggs per clutch in a given season. The eggs will vary in size depending on the size of the female that deposited the eggs and the size of the clutch. The eggs can take anywhere from 90 to over 400 days to hatch. The entire reproduction cycle will, of course, vary depending on the geographic and topographic location of any particular population.

Wild leopard tortoises often have pyramided shells, a condition seen in most other tortoise species only in captivity.

# Range Maps of Sulcat

These maps give a approximate natural ranges for the sulcata tortoise
(this page) and the leopard tortoise (facing page). Note that these tortoises
do not seem to overlap in range. Of course, more research could reveal

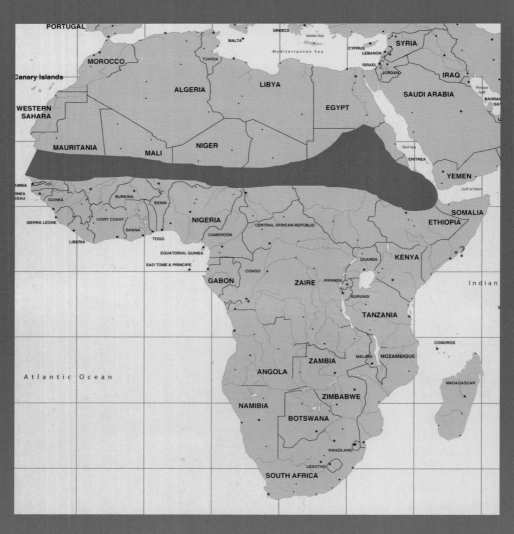

# nd Leopard Tortoises

hidden populations of either species outside of the currently known range.
The population density of these turtles will vary across the range according
to the local habitat and human population.

These maps are adapted from Iverson, J. B. A *Revised Checklist With Distribution Maps of Turtles of the World.* 1992 J.P. Iverson Publishing. They are
used with permission of the publisher.

# Chapter 2

# Pet Considerations

**W**hen thinking of adding any new pet to the household, it is wise to compile a list of various things you will need to consider once the pet is in the house. You need to know whether this is actually the right pet for you, after thinking about what is required by that pet in terms of housing and providing all of its basic needs, including those needs in times of emergency, such as if the pet requires medical attention. Tortoises are no different, and you should think carefully and realistically before you acquire one.

## Think Before You Buy

**When considering one or both of these fantastic tortoises it becomes relatively clear that a leopard tortoise or sulcata is not for everyone. These tortoises require a little more care than the average pet. In many cases they require more work than a pet dog or a cat, even though the work entailed in providing that care can be minimized with some good planning. Think carefully and realistically before bringing home one of these tortoises.**

## Before You Get A Tortoise

When you decide that a leopard or sulcata tortoise would be a pleasant addition to the household, you must address many aspects related to keeping the tortoise. The most basic consideration should be to fully research and plan for the tortoise before you actually bring it home. The better the research and the better the planning, the easier and less stressful the process of adding such a pet to the household will be. It is much easier and safer to the well-being of the tortoise and the tortoise keeper to have everything that is needed and ready to go before the tortoise is actually brought home than to find out after the fact that there you lack a component missing that could be vital to the tortoise's health or very survival.

## The Basics

Some of the more important points that you will need to take into account before obtaining a tortoise are housing, environmental needs, feeding, and finding a tortoise-experienced veterinarian. These are the things that should be in order before you add a tortoise to the household. If you consider all the essential items before the tortoise arrives, you will avoid the need to frantically scramble when you discover there is some missing piece.

A few special points have to be mentioned when considering these two tortoises, and especially the sulcata. As already pointed out, this tortoise can reach weights of over 200 lbs (90.7 kg). The sulcata is a very active tortoise, so you need to provide special and sturdy accommodations. While it does take roughly 10 to 15 years for sulcatas to reach this weight, under ideal conditions they can get to be over 100 pounds (45.4 kg) in as little as 5 years. If you need to keep the tortoise indoors, this adds a totally new dimension to the problem of dealing with this particular animal. Also remember that these tortoises may live 50 years or more and will require your care (or someone else's) for all of that time. It is a wise idea before proceeding to be sure you give the keeping of a sulcata very careful thought and consideration.

## Indoors or Outdoors

When considering accommodations for the tortoise, you must decide whether the animal is going to be housed outdoors or indoors and how much space you can or should allot to it. There is of course such a thing as too little space, but there can also be too much space, depending on the size of the tortoise when obtained and on how big the tortoise will get. A secure enclosure is very important in both the indoor and outdoor housing situations. For the indoor tortoise, you must account for safety from other pets and unsupervised children. For the outdoor pet, you must consider these same items in addition to protection from the elements and wild animals. Once the enclosure has been determined, you need to plan out the furnishings such as substrate, rocks, logs, plantings, and other elements.

With a plan for the enclosure in place, you have to think about the tortoise's living. Tortoises are what some refer to as poikilotherms—"cold-blooded" to most people. This does not mean that the animals blood is cold, but refers to the fact that for the most part the tortoise is dependent on its surroundings to provide a proper body temperature that allows the animal's metabolism to function properly. Supplemental heating is

Plan carefully before buying a baby tortoise—it won't stay that small for long.

usually required to maintain a good body temperature during times when the tortoise is not able do this on its own. In line with temperature, these two tortoises need hydration and humidity. Hydration is probably the second most important component in the tortoise's metabolism and development, so you will have to understand this before obtaining your tortoise.

## Food

Once the enclosure is set up and ready, the next step is to decide what foods and feeding schedule you can provide. In the current age of keeping pet tortoises, there are many options here. An all-plant-based diet can be provided, but there are also some very good manufactured diets that are also available. In the case of the leopard and the sulcata, you can use a combination of the two, and this might even be beneficial. The important point is to find out what items the tortoises need and where you can obtain them.

## Veterinary Care

Next you must plan on what you will do in the event the tortoise gets sick or is injured. The minimum

Both leopards and sulcatas thrive best in spacious outdoor enclosures, which will likely take up most of your yard.

*Sulcata and Leopard Tortoises*

requirement for this plan is to get a list of veterinarians in the area and try to find some veterinarians who specialize in—or are at least well versed in—the care and treatment of tortoises. The veterinarians who fall under this classification are usually considered exotic pet veterinarians and are usually listed as such. It is a good idea to have the name or names of veterinarians before you actually need one, because it makes an emergency easier to deal with. With the leopard and sulcata there might be a time when you will need a vet who will actually make house calls because of the size some of these tortoises attain.

## Obtaining a Tortoise

The preceding considerations will be covered in greater detail later on in the guide. These thoughts are given to present a general idea of what to expect before bringing home a leopard tortoise or sulcata. With all this in mind the task of acquiring the new tortoise is the next step.

### Pet Stores

In general, whenever the thought of obtaining a pet comes to mind the local pet shop is usually the first place that most people turn to. There are many types of pet shops that are available, and each has its advantages as well as disadvantages. The variety of shops can extend from the small local pet shop to the national chain stores. A pet tortoise can usually be found in one, if not all, of these outlets.

Here are some tips to keep in mind when considering any pet shop for purchasing your African spurred or leopard tortoise. A good indication of the quality of the store you are

## Ouch!

The risks of being bitten by one of these tortoises is minimal. Bites are almost always part of a feeding response. The tortoise will sniff the intended morsel and then proceed to take a bite if it smells good— hands that have just touched tortoise food will smell like tortoise food! The greatest risks are having bare feet or open-toed shoes while maintaining the tortoise enclosure and offering food by hand. These tortoises—especially adult sulcatas—do have a very strong bite and can inflict pain and damage but only if the keeper is careless.

dealing with is, of course, the first impression. It is a good idea to take notice of the enclosures in which the animals are kept to be sure they are generally clean. Pay particular attention to see that the water bowls are filled with clean fresh water. Look to see that the enclosures are relatively spacious and that the animals are not overcrowded; check also that the enclosures do not contain more than one type of tortoise. A shop that presents itself well, is well organized, and gives the appearance of being well maintained is providing a good indication that it places an importance on the animals in their care.

Breeders produce large numbers of sulcatas each year.

**Local Pet Shop** To begin with, the local privately owned pet shop can be a good place to obtain a tortoise because the shop owner has a vested interest in the sale. This works to the benefit of the new tortoise owner in that the owner of the shop is usually working to solidify the business relationship with the new tortoise keeper to encourage the keeper to continue coming back for food, supplies, and other necessities. It is for this reason that there seems to be a little more personal attention given to the customer. If there are any problems, the private shop owner is usually willing to work a little harder in order to resolve those problems for this very reason.

The major disadvantage of purchasing a tortoise from the small shop is that it would seem that the majority of small shops concentrate on the more common pets like dogs, cats, fish, and birds. Therefore the knowledge base for the keeping of tortoises is sometimes limited, but there are exceptions. In the small local pet shop, it is also not uncommon to see several different tortoises housed together, which is usually not accepted by many tortoise keepers as a good practice.

Buy a tortoise only from a pet store that houses its animals properly.

**Reptile Specialty Shop** Another type of privately owned pet shop is the reptile specialty shop. This kind of pet shop deals with exotic pets and in many cases almost exclusively with reptiles and amphibians. It is this kind of specialty type shop that is most likely the best resource in obtaining a new tortoise; in addition to having many of the advantages of a small general-pet shop, it also includes the benefit of a good knowledge base on the animals you are seeking. Many of the shopkeepers who own or operate such pet shops started out as reptile enthusiasts themselves, so they are well in tune with the needs of their customers. This is a great benefit to you, because it usually means that the shop owner knows your needs, which makes purchasing and keeping one of these tortoises easier. With the proper guidance it is also less likely for any necessities to be missed or any unnecessary items to be added.

It is in the specialty shop that you can be relatively certain that the tortoise you are getting is healthy and well cared for. It is also because these shops usually have such a good knowledge base that it is not very likely you will come across substandard animals or unacceptable husbandry practices such as housing different animals together in the same enclosure or overcrowded conditions. There is one disadvantage here and that is because these kinds of pet shops are so specialized they are not very common, usually being found only around the bigger cities. However, many of these shops also do business either through the mail or over the Internet.

**Large Chain Pet Shops** The last type of pet shop that is going to be mentioned here is the big chain or department store-type of pet shop. It is in this kind of shop you will usually find the best prices and convenience, but you really have to know what you are looking for with both the tortoise in mind and the supplies required to maintain that tortoise. The salespeople who usually work in chain stores,

## Inherit the Tortoise

It is always important to understand that when obtaining any new pet, you must provide for its care through the course of its life. With a tortoise, that commitment could last well over 50 years! You should make provisions for the time you may no longer be able to care for your pet.

even though well intentioned, are usually lacking in a strong knowledge base. Many of the larger chain stores have tried to address this by providing training classes for the workers who take care of the different departments, including the reptile department. Another disadvantage of the larger stores is that the selection is usually limited in both the livestock and the supplies.

## Breeders and Reptile Shows

As the hobby of keeping reptiles grew in both popularity and scope it was only a matter of time until the advent of reptile shows (also called herp shows, reptile expos, and herp expos). Reptile shows began to make their appearance in the 1990s. Since that time, many of these shows have sprung up the world over and have gained very wide popularity and acceptance. The reptile show is a kind of swap meet where amphibians, reptiles, and supplies relating to these animals are sold and traded by all forms of businesses in the world of herpetoculture (which is the general term for the keeping and breeding of amphibians and reptiles) along with the private hobbyist. These swap meets can be as small as a few tables at a local school gym in a small community to as large as hundreds of tables at a large

## Ask a Turtle Club Member

With a little research you can find many more sources beyond the pet shop for obtaining African tortoises. In fact, you are more likely to find these tortoises at some of the following suggested sources more so than in any pet shop because they are no longer imported into the United States and not very commonly imported into other countries. You will usually be able to find your leopard tortoise or sulcata at a reptile show, tortoise breeder, or animal rescue organization.

A good starting place to find any of these particular outlets is to consult your local turtle and tortoise club or organization. Information about these groups can usually be found at a pet shop, on a local library bulletin board, or on the Internet. The members of local turtle and tortoise clubs are usually more than happy and willing to provide help and guidance to other tortoise keepers because most of them follow this hobby with a passion and usually enjoy the interaction with others having similar interests. The people in these clubs will know reputable sources of tortoises and be able to put you in touch with them. Some members likely will be breeders themselves.

Reptile rescue organizations often have sulcatas in need of good homes.

convention center in a major city. In many of the larger shows, people literally come from all over the world to buy, sell, and sometimes trade amphibians, reptiles, and related supplies. This can be quite a sight to see for the person who is just beginning to get involved in the keeping of tortoises. At the smaller shows you usually have fewer vendors and a smaller selection of animals, but it is much easier to get information on a personal level from the seller than it is at the large and usually more crowded expos.

If you can find the species of tortoise you are looking for at a small show, it is here that you will also usually get your best deal in both price and quality of tortoise. Unfortunately, it is also at the reptile shows that your risk of being taken advantage of can also increase, so it is always a good idea to go with someone who is familiar with the environment. Many of the vendors, as mentioned earlier, are private individuals who do not always attend the shows or attend the shows only sporadically. If you do purchase your tortoise from such a person, be sure to get as much information from that person as you can. You should get as much information as you can about the tortoise in terms of its care and history, and also be sure to get contact information from the vendor. That way if anything does go wrong or you have any more questions about your new tortoise, you will have someone to turn to. Most of the vendors at reptile shows are the breeders of the species they are selling. There are incidental breeders who have the occasional pair that breed for them on occasion. There are

small backyard breeders who have taken their passion a bit further, to the point where they supplement their hobby through the sale of some of the offspring they produce. Then there are the large-scale commercial breeders who actually make a living at breeding tortoises. All of these are people in the hobby of keeping tortoises who have taken the passion of keeping these animals to the level of reproducing them for fun and, in some cases, profit. It also should be mentioned that not every breeder participates in the reptile shows.

Outside of the reptile shows, contacts for these breeders can be found in reptile magazines or on the Internet. But the most popular and successful way of finding a good tortoise breeder is by word of mouth and networking. Among the different levels of tortoise breeders, the incidental breeder becomes your best opportunity for getting a good tortoise at a good price. The offspring produced by the incidental tortoise breeder are usually the result of

## Checklist of Things You Need

**Here's a quick list of things you need before you bring home a tortoise.**

- **An appropriately-sized, secure enclosure**
- **Proper heating and lighting (and temperature controls)**
- **Suitable substrate or bedding**
- **A water bowl**
- **A supply of the correct food**
- **The contact information for a veterinarian familiar with tortoises**

**Remember that before you bring a tortoise home, you should have its enclosure already set up and should be sure that you have a proper temperature and humidity to guarantee the continued good health of the tortoise you have chosen.**

a pet tortoise depositing eggs and producing offspring when the owner was really not trying to get the pet tortoise to produce offspring. These babies usually get the greatest care, because they are personal pets of the breeders. Another benefit is that the breeders are usually not very concerned about the price of the offspring, because they are not doing it as a business. Their main concern is usually finding a good home for the juveniles that they care so much about rather than making money. The only drawback to obtaining your tortoise from this source is finding the person. Obtaining a contact for such a person is almost exclusively by word of mouth and is usually a matter of being at the right place at the right time.

An easier source to find than the incidental breeder is the backyard tortoise breeder. These individuals try to have their pets breed as a means to provide supplemental income for their hobby, but their operation is still on a scale small enough to provide individual care for the offspring that are produced. This type of tortoise breeder usually advertises in the local tortoise club newsletters in addition to various bulletin boards on the Internet. They also produce offspring on a more consistent basis. You can still get a good level of service and value—but you will notice an obvious increase in average price.

The next step up from the incidental breeder is the large-scale commercial tortoise breeder. Many of these breeders produce tortoise offspring on such a large scale that it is virtually impossible to provide individual care for all of the juvenile tortoises. This might be seen as a bad thing, but this allows the breeder to sell the tortoises at a better price than the backyard breeder.

> Because the exportation and importation of African tortoises is heavily regulated, most of the leopards and sulcatas in the hobby are captive bred.

Because of the experience that this type of keeper has developed over time, the large-scale tortoise breeder has built his or her business on a gradual scale to produce large numbers of healthy offspring efficiently. Usually the commercial tortoise breeder has taken a long time to develop the operation, and in doing so, has also developed a good knowledge base along with a good reputation. Many large-scale breeders have a company name that can be found in reptile publications, online reptile forums, and their own websites. The large-scale tortoise breeder can have some distinct advantages as a source for the leopard tortoise and sulcata. As mentioned earlier, they have usually been around for a long time, so it is easy to do a background check. Also, they have usually turned their passion for keeping tortoises into business because they not only like dealing with the tortoises they keep but they also seem to enjoy the interaction with the other keepers. Good tortoise breeders will gladly answer your questions because they know exactly what it is like when they need help and seek information from other fellow tortoise keepers.

Avoid purchasing a tortoise that appears listless and has half-closed or sunken eyes.

*Sulcata and Leopard Tortoises*

# Ethical Questions

Should tortoises be taken out of the wild? This is a highly controversial topic, and one that is well worth thinking about. Many of the tortoises you see in the pet trade are wild-caught, although the trend is slowly changing. These animals are sometimes collected in vast numbers, and their capture probably does adversely impact the wild populations. Many people believe this is wrong and speak quite harshly against the availability and purchase of the wild-caught tortoises. If you too have strong feelings against the taking of animals out of the wild, don't purchase one. By purchasing a wild-caught animal you are not saving it, but you are perpetuating the market and opening up another slot for yet another wild-caught tortoise.

This is not a clear-cut issue, because you cannot have captive-born tortoises without a founding captive population to produce those offspring. The founding population is made up of the wild-caught tortoises that produce the captive-bred tortoises. It would be a good idea that wild-caught tortoises be regulated as far as being restricted to being kept only by those tortoise keepers who have developed a good amount of experience so as to increase the chances of survival of the founding stock in captivity. Additionally, if the local people in the tortoises' home ranges can capture for home-range farming and sell some of the tortoises, they may view them and their habitat as a valuable resource instead of something to be ploughed under for farmland or other development.

This is an issue that the reptile hobby, biologists, conservation groups, and government officials need to look at together. It is up to you what route you choose to take when obtaining your tortoise. Keep in mind that currently the chances of coming across a wild-caught leopard tortoise are small and the chances of coming across a wild-caught sulcata are smaller yet.

## Rescue Organizations

Finally, there is one resource for acquiring a tortoise that is unique to sulcatas and occasionally leopard tortoises. Animal rescue services are organizations that take in unwanted pets. Many of these organizations specialize in turtles and tortoises. Some people do not realize the specialized requirements of these tortoise and end up having to give them up for adoption because they are unable to meet those requirements. Many of these tortoises that cannot be properly cared for make fantastic pets if you know what you are getting into. You can find tortoise rescues by contacting your local animal shelter, searching on the Internet, and looking at the Resource section of this guide.

## Selecting the New Tortoise

Once you know where your new tortoise is going to come from it is a good idea to have some notion of what exactly you are looking for in an individual leopard or sulcata tortoise. In this case, you might be wondering what a good, healthy leopard tortoise or sulcata looks like.

### Wild-Caught Versus Captive-Bred

There are two main origins for tortoises and herps in general. They can be either wild-caught or captive-bred. Wild-caught (often abbreviated WC) tortoises are animals that are taken out of the wild. Captive-bred (often abbreviated CB) tortoises were hatched in captivity by the breeder. Captive-bred tortoises are the preferred pets for various reasons. In the case of leopards and sulcatas, you are more like to encounter captive-bred individuals than wild-caught ones. Exportation of the sulcata is no longer allowed because of protections within its native countries. There are severe restrictions on the number of leopard tortoises that can be exported because of protective quotas in place within their native countries. Additionally, the US has banned the importation of sulcatas, leopards, and a few other African tortoises because of the potential for these tortoises to carry ticks that will spread heartwater disease, a deadly disease of cattle. Importation restrictions are fairly recent, so there is a chance of coming across examples of these species that were originally wild-caught and have been in captivity for a while, but this is not very common.

Wild-caught tortoises are usually lower in price, but often you end up paying for that lower price in both time and money. Wild-caught tortoises are notorious for being heavy carriers of internal parasites and diseases that eventually lead to problems. While they can live with these problems in the wild, the stress of being yanked out of their natural habitat and thrown into an unnatural environment leads to their ability to deal with these

# Warning Signs

There are certain key points to look for in selecting a healthy tortoise. Should you see a tortoise displaying one or more of the following signs, it would be best to avoid that particular animal.

- **Inactive and not moving very much**
- **Sunken or closed eyes**
- **Light weight**
- **Watery eyes or runny nose**
- **Loose or bloody feces**
- **Soft shell**
- **Caked feces around the back end of the shell**
- **Limbs not functioning properly**

pathogens being severely impaired. At that point, the wild-caught tortoise's health starts to decline, invariably leading to a veterinarian visit, a sizable veterinarian bill, and sometimes a dead tortoise. So any savings you might realize by purchasing the wild-caught tortoise is pretty much exhausted, along with much more money than the initial cost. Wild-caught tortoises very often are also more difficult to acclimate or adjust to captivity. It's only fair to mention that there are some minor advantages to acquiring a wild-caught tortoise. If you are able to acclimate the wild-caught tortoise, you can usually start with adult animals. If you intend to eventually breed your pet, starting off with an adult can reduce the amount of time you have to wait for the tortoise to reach sexual maturity. Another point in terms of breeding is that with wild-caught tortoises you can be relatively sure they are not related, so the acquisition of wild-caught tortoises can be beneficial in terms of genetic diversity if the final goal is the breeding of your pets.

It is needless to say that the better tortoise to acquire is, of course, the captive-bred and raised tortoise. The captive-bred tortoise will present the fewest problems and the greatest rewards. In most cases, captive-bred tortoises are free of parasites, are acclimated to captivity, and are used to eating easily obtainable food. The only real disadvantage in obtaining the captive-bred tortoise is the amount of time it usually takes the tortoise to reach maturity, but as mentioned earlier, the reward of raising that tortoise from hatchling to adult is very satisfying.

## Signs of a Healthy Tortoise

Regardless of where the tortoise comes from, there are certain things to be on the lookout for when actually selecting the tortoise you have in mind. The most important item is that you are looking for the tortoise that is active and alert. When looking at a leopard tortoise, this can be difficult, because leopard tortoises are notoriously shy. If you can see the tortoise eating and/or drinking, those are usually good signs that it is a strong, healthy, and well-acclimated animal.

You also want to look for signs of dehydration such as sunken eyes or excessively loose skin around the head or limbs. Looking

Check the weight of any tortoise you are planning to purchase. A healthy tortoise will feel heavy for its size.

at the eyes, you want to see them fully open, with a kind of sparkle to them in addition to their fully filling the eye socket. This is another tell-tale indicator as to the general health of the tortoise.

When you look at the nostrils of the tortoise they should be dry and clear. A common problem among tortoises in general is a runny or wet nose, but this is not very common in captive-bred leopards and sulcatas. Runny or wet noses can be an indication of many different problems, so it is best to avoid any tortoises that show any such signs.

The leopard tortoise is generally shy by nature—as are very young sulcatas—so this can sometimes make assessing the health of hatchlings difficult. If the temperature is warm and comfortable you will usually see these tortoises running about in an animated

fashion. When being picked up, they should remain very active and alert. You should have no trouble looking for the above-mentioned indicators. A more in-depth health assessment will be covered in the chapter on health care. If the general signs of good health mentioned above are absent from the animals you are looking at and they are very inactive or to not coming out of their shells, it is probably a good idea that you look for another tortoise.

## Initial Checkup

Even if you have followed the preceding suggestions, it is always a good idea to take your new tortoise for a preliminary vet checkup regardless of how healthy the outward appearance might be. Scheduling a veterinarian visit as soon as you bring the new tortoise home is a very important step no matter the origin of the tortoise. Being captive-bred does not guarantee that the tortoise is free of problems. Even the most well-intentioned keeper or breeder occasionally has problems that might go unnoticed, so the veterinarian visit is recommended so that any of these small unnoticed problems can be dealt with before they become large noticeable problems.

The most important item the veterinarian needs to look for is any form of parasites, both internal and external. Parasites can cause serious problems if they go unchecked. It is during the stress of transitioning from one keeper to the next that any parasite load will have the opportunity to gain the upper hand and create a physical problem. With the conclusion of the vet visit and a clean bill of health, you are now ready to face the basic upkeep of your new tortoise.

# Chapter 3

# Housing

There are two basic options for housing either the sulcata or leopard tortoise: indoors or outdoors. Outdoors is always preferred, but for many reasons this is not always an option. Some owners may live in a geographical location where it is not safe to house a tortoise outdoors, usually for reasons of seasonal temperature variations, other environmental conditions, the presence of harmful predators, or some combination of these factors. These obstacles can be overcome during most if not all of the year with careful planning and implementation, but in the case of an adult sulcata outdoor housing can be both very expensive and space consuming.

## Heat and Hydration

The leopard tortoise and sulcata are dependent on their environment to maintain body temperatures in the right range to adequately digest food and maintain normal activity. When keeping tortoises this is a key point, because if the keeper does not maintain temperatures in the proper range, the tortoise will starve to death regardless of the availability of food and water. It is for this reason that it is recommended that you take a little time after you have your tortoise set up and observe it in the environment you have provided. You are going to have to establish the balance that will work for your situation. The balance that you are looking for is to provide a temperature that will keep the tortoise on an active schedule and to provide the proper amount and type of food and water that will support that activity in addition to providing a good regular growth rate.

Proper hydration is critical to the successfull keeping of leopards and sulcatas, even though they inhabit arid areas.

Proper heat and hydration are stressed so strongly because these two components have an immediate and direct bearing on the entire functioning of the metabolism and determine whether or not the turtle will thrive. Deficiencies or imbalances in one or both of these areas are the most frequent causes of problems among captive tortoises. Bear in mind that there are not only differences among the different types of tortoises but also among different individuals. For this reason, it is important to provide as much of a choice among all the components involved in maintaining your tortoise in captivity as you possibly can.

The temperature is the most important component of housing leopard tortoises and sulcatas. By providing an ambient temperature range of 75 to 100°F (23.9 to 37.8°C) you are giving the tortoise the ability to regulate its own temperature according to its needs. Both the leopard tortoise and the sulcata come from relatively warm and harsh environments. If the temperatures should drop too low, as it does in the cooler seasons, the tortoise will stop eating and go into a resting state called estivation, which is much like hibernation. In the wild this usually coincides with the unavailability of plants and other food that occurs during that period. More important than that, it allows the tortoise to survive the season when the temperatures are too low for the tortoise to process or digest the food. This would be the situation in the southern range of the leopard tortoise.

There is also the opposite extreme: temperatures that climb so high that there is the possibility that the tortoise can overheat. During the periods where the temperatures are that high, the tortoise will seek refuge in an area where it can escape those temperatures and will again estivate until favorable conditions return. The sulcata deals with those extreme conditions in the desert habitat by digging extensively long and deep burrows to escape the high desert temperatures. Because this is a conditioned survival trait, sulcatas will do—or try to do— the same in captivity if adequate housing is not provided.

When adding supplemental heating, you should note that this tends to lead to an increase in dehydration. The increased heat causes the enclosure to dry out, and you must take precautions against this. This is a concern even in regions of higher humidity, because the heating of the enclosure will cause drying within it. The tortoise then runs the risk of becoming dehydrated because there is an increase in the loss of body fluid through respiration or normal breathing. With hatchling and yearling tortoises, this is especially critical because of their relatively small size and body mass. It is believed that dehydration is one of the primary causes for young tortoises to fail to thrive.

When the tortoise is first brought home you should watch it very carefully. By placing the water bowl in a corner or along the perimeter of the enclosure you can be relatively certain that the tortoise is going to encounter the dish in its travels, because most tortoises initially will pace the perimeter. Watch to be sure the tortoise is actually doing such pacing. At first it is a good practice to soak the tortoise daily or every other day to make certain it has the opportunity to take in water. You can soak your tortoise in a clean cat litter pan, plastic sweaterbox, or any similar container. For larger tortoises, this is not as critical as it is with smaller tortoises, so once or twice a week is sufficient if the tortoise is eating. Over time, you will see that the tortoise knows where to find its water.

Hobbyists often keep sulcatas and leopards indoors for their first few years of life.

## Indoor Enclosures

If you decide to situate your tortoise's enclosure indoors, the next consideration is the size of the enclosure, and that will depend on the size of the tortoise and the space you have available. The size of the tortoise and the space you are providing for it to live in are probably the two most important decisions when thinking of a good home for your tortoise. You will also have to consider what you will make the enclosure out of, how to heat and light it, and many other factors. If you have a hatchling, you will have to plan to expand and modify the enclosure as the tortoise grows.

## Enclosure Size

Bigger is not always better when you are thinking of the size of the enclosure for one of these tortoises. You should not place a hatchling leopard tortoise or sulcata into a one-acre corral; if you did, you would most likely lose it. More importantly, in such a large area you could not properly control the environmental conditions that are necessary for the survival of the tortoise at that size. At the same time, you obviously should not place an adult sulcata within a small enclosure.

As a general guide line, use this formula for your enclosure's minimal dimensions: 10x in length by 5x in width by 3x in height where x is the length of the tortoise determined by measuring the tortoise straight across the plastron (This is sometimes called the straight carapace length, or SCL). So, a 10-inch (25.4-cm) sulcata should have an enclosure measuring roughly 100 inches long, 50 inches wide and 30 inches high (254 cm by 127 cm by 76.2 cm). Keep in mind that when you start with these dimensions you have to consider how much control over the environmental conditions you can safely maintain. If more control is required, you are going to need an enclosure that is neither too small nor too large. For hatchling tortoises of these species, some examples of starter enclosures that usually come close to the previously mentioned dimensions are a 20- to 30-gallon (75.7- to 113.6-l) aquarium or similar glass enclosure or plastic sweater box. All of these enclosures have their advantages and disadvantages.

## Enclosure Materials

If you use a glass, plastic, or other clear enclosure, you have to observe the tortoise to

## Cold-Blooded Life

**Tortoises are reptiles and as such are dependent on their environment to provide a body temperature that will allow them to maintain a good metabolism and normal bodily functions. These animals require a specific temperature range in their environment because they are not physically capable of maintaining that temperature in their own bodies.**

If you house your tortoises in a glass enclosure, monitor the temperature carefully. Note that alfalfa pellets are not an appropriate substrate.

make certain it is not always trying to go through the wall. Because it can see through the wall of the enclosure, some tortoises don't realize the barrier is there and keep trying to get out. Most tortoises adapt well to clear enclosures, but some do not. If you find that your tortoise is always trying to get out you might be able to remedy the situation by placing a dark border on the bottom 3 or 4 inches (7.6-10.2 cm) of the enclosure wall. You can use a solid-colored tape or you can paint a border on the outside walls of the enclosure.

One other point of caution is that glass or high-walled enclosures can retain heat. This can be both an advantage and a disadvantage, depending on the ambient temperatures. In cooler climates or households, the retention of heat is an advantage because it makes it easier to maintain a temperature gradient. In a warmer climate or household, there is an obvious disadvantage in that the retained heat can do harm to your tortoise if the temperatures are not properly monitored and controlled. If you use a glass enclosure, you must take extreme caution when positioning the enclosure in relation to the sun. The glass enclosure acts as a heat trap in direct sunlight, which can quickly overheat the tortoise. Do not place a glass enclosure in direct sunlight unless it is your intention to use the sunlight as a heat source. This can be done, but it is very risky because it is so difficult to control the heat that is produced in this manner.

You can take precautions to avoid overheating by using an enclosure that is of adequate size so as to allow sufficient air circulation. Good air circulation can also be provided by using an enclosure that has low walls. There are many glass enclosures that are made today specifically for use in maintaining reptiles and even more specifically for tortoises. These enclosures generally have better ventilation than a fish tank, so overheating is not as likely.

Many people prefer plastic enclosures made of sweater boxes or under-bed blanket boxes because of their availability and low cost. Another advantage is that they are translucent rather than transparent. The translucency does not allow the tortoise to see out, eliminating the chance that it will continually try to escape through the wall. These types of enclosures can be found in almost any hardware store, discount store, or department store. Many of them are usually constructed with low sides so heat is not easily retained; as a result there is less chance of the tortoise's becoming overheated. As mentioned earlier, low sides can also be a disadvantage because it may also be difficult to keep the enclosure warm enough for the tortoise.

Both types of enclosures mentioned so far have the added benefit of already being waterproof. This makes them easy to clean without the concern of whether the enclosure is going to rot and fall apart or not. The tortoise's normal bodily functions also provide moisture that can be very destructive if the enclosure is not properly protected and cleaned. With other types of enclosures, you may have the added work of providing a waterproof finish. The glass or plastic enclosure makes it easier to maintain the humidity that these tortoises need without any great concern for rot, mold, or mildew.

## Custom Enclosures

While plastic box enclosures can have their benefits, they are usually not very attractive as far as furniture goes. This is where a custom-built enclosure comes in. It can be as elaborate as a decorated cabinet or as simple as a tortoise table, as it is commonly called—really nothing more than a wooden box. In cooler climates, a full enclosure is a more practical choice because it makes heat

## Size Issues

Both the leopard tortoise and the sulcata present unique challenges because of their size as adults and the fact that they don't normally estivate. Housing must be provided throughout the year regardless of the climate in which they are kept. In the case of adults, those accommodations should be quite large. For first few years, the two tortoises are smaller and can be treated like most other tortoises when kept indoors or out.

# Enclosure Size

**To figure out the size of the enclosure you will need for your tortoise, you can use this simple formula to determine the minmum space requirements:**

**length = 10x**

**width = 5x**

**height = 3 x**

**Where x equals the length of the tortoise.**

retention easier. A closed cabinet-type enclosure is a good choice in these areas. In a warmer zone, the tortoise table would be the most likely choice for an enclosure, because retaining heat is usually not a problem.

The tortoise table has been the enclosure of choice for maintaining tortoises indoors for well over 100 years. The enclosure is very basic in design in that it has the appearance of nothing more than a bookcase that has been laid on its back with the shelves removed. In actuality, this very idea has been employed by many keepers but is not recommended, because bookcases usually use very thin wood for the backing, and as a floor this material does not hold up very well to the activities of the average sulcata. If you are the handy type, you can easily build a tortoise table from scratch using shelving material and three-quarter-inch (1.9-cm) thick plywood for the bottom. If you're not very handy, many lumber sellers are willing to cut the wood you need to your specified dimensions for a minimal charge. Some sellers will also construct the enclosure for yet another (but less minimal) charge. A few might even also put a finish on the enclosure for still another charge. It should be pretty clear that you can save yourself a good deal of money in the construction of your tortoise table by completing as many steps of the building process as you can. If done properly, this can actually be part of the fun in the process of tortoise keeping. If you do decide to tackle the construction of your own tortoise table, here are some points that should be considered in order to make the task easier.

Ideally, the table should be constructed of a hardwood such as oak or a plywood having an oak veneer. This will last the life of the tortoise if it is constructed properly, but the leopard and the sulcata will outgrow this type of enclosure long before that. The drawback with this kind of construction is that most hardwoods are going to be relatively expensive, and some can be difficult to work with. Pine, a softwood, is an easy wood to work with and is also less expensive. The only caution about using pine wood is that you have to be sure that it is properly finished because of its softness. Particle board is less expensive but is not recommended because if it is not sealed properly it tends to fall apart if it is exposed to any kind of moisture. When considering the flooring of the enclosure, it is a good idea to construct the floor of plywood because it is much more durable than solid pine. It also allows you to provide a flatter surface for easier construction; that's because plywood is available in wide sheets, whereas unworked pine usually is available in boards no wider than 12 inches, and those boards—which are not always as flat as you'd like them—have to be joined side by side.

The sides of the tortoise table can be constructed of standard-width pine boards, depending on the height of the sides that are desired. A good height for the sides would be 12 inches (30.5 cm), which is a sufficient height to allow a good layer of substrate in addition to providing enough height to keep a young tortoise from escaping. You can always make the sides higher or lower as you deem necessary.

Once the tortoise table is constructed, the next step is to provide a good protective coating to the surfaces that are going to be exposed to any kind of moisture. As a covering you can use a plastic laminate or veneer or a liquid coating such as paint or plastic. A solid covering is much more durable than a liquid covering but is also much more difficult to apply and if not applied properly will actually do more damage than good because it tends to trap moisture under the surface. One of the easier durable coatings to apply is polyurethane, which is a type of liquid plastic. Polyurethane does tend to be soft, but if enough layers are applied with care it can last for many years. A suggested course of action would be to sand the interior of the enclosure to a very smooth finish and then apply 10 to 15 coats on the inside of the enclosure. It is not

Most hobbyists who house tortoises indoors build their own enclosures. This is one of the author's leopard tortoise pens.

# Substrates and Impaction

It is commonly believed that many loose substrates are hazardous to use for smaller tortoises because of the risk of impaction. Impaction of the digestive system occurs when the tortoise ingests substrate that blocks the digestive system and the tortoise can no longer digest or pass its food. It eventually dies because of a build-up of fluid and food that it cannot pass. Why tortoises ingest the substrate is a topic of much debate, but it is believed that if all of the environmental conditions are favorable and the tortoise is well fed in addition to well hydrated, impaction is of little or no concern.

necessary to apply more than three or four coats on the outside. This might sound like a great deal of work and time, but each coat dries and can be recoated in roughly 30 to 60 minutes at 70 to 80°F (21.1 to 26.7°C). (Drying times vary, so check the container in which a particular finish comes to determine its drying time.) High humidity will increase that time. Allow the finish to dry for a day or two to be sure the polyurethane is totally dry even though it might seem sufficiently dry a few hours after the last coat. You now have a tortoise table that is ready for the addition of a substrate and any other furnishings that you need or desire.

## Substrate

At the very least, a substrate that will supply a decent footing for the tortoise should be provided. Some commonly used substrates are sand, soil, a sand and soil mixture, pine bark mulch, cypress mulch, aspen bedding, and many kinds of hay or grass clippings. These substrates can be used alone or in combination with each other to add variety to both the appearance and the environment the tortoise is exposed to. Both the leopard tortoise and the sulcata come from relatively harsh environments that usually consist mostly of hard soil or sand for the most part. It is for this reason that a substrate of soil and/or sand seems most appropriate for the setup housing these tortoises.

Regardless of the substrate that you do decide to use, be sure that is free of any kind of chemicals or contamination, such as animal waste. This is mentioned because it is not uncommon to use substrates or rocks that you would find outdoors to furnish your enclosure, and this is perfectly acceptable. You just have to make sure you know where the material is coming from and that it is relatively clean. If using loam, leaf litter, sand, or dirt from outdoors, try to collect it from areas that are well drained. Also, try to collect it from

Sand or a sand and soil mix is a fine substrate for leopard tortoises.

areas where the chance of the substrate's being exposed to animal waste or chemicals such as fertilizers or chemical runoff is least likely. Some examples of chemical runoff would be oil, gas, and automobile coolant.

Many of these substrates are readily available for purchase at any hardware store, garden supply center, feed store, or landscaping outlet. Purchasing the substrate in bulk will usually eliminate the concern you might have for collecting material that might be tainted with anything that could be harmful to your pet. This is the much safer—although more expensive—way to go when choosing a substrate.

There are some additional cautions when choosing a substrate. Tortoise keepers are sometimes worried about the hazards of impaction, the internal blockage that occurs if a tortoise consumes too much substrate. This should not be of any concern if you have a healthy tortoise and it is kept in a healthy environment. What goes in will usually come out in a healthy active tortoise. There are also some beddings that are not recommended as substrates. Pine shavings, cedar shavings, and any kind of consumable pellet (such as alfalfa pellets used for rabbit food) should not be used as a substrate for various reasons.

## Furnishings

Once you select a substrate, the next items to add are furnishings such as a hiding place, rocks, and logs. The hiding place provides a place for the tortoise to rest and feel secure. While leopard tortoises are not known for burrowing, the sulcata is. The hiding place for the sulcata is essential because larger sulcatas can be quite destructive while trying to burrow in order to feel secure. Giving them a hiding place makes them less prone to digging their own burrows. The rocks or logs provide visual barriers, which both break up the line of sight and provide exercise. It is important not to overdo the furnishings. Tortoises in general do not seem to pay much attention to furnishings apart from viewing them as obstacles, and these African tortoises are no different. The idea is to provide furnishings that are practical from the standpoint of the tortoise and not place so many furnishings that valuable space is taken away from the tortoise.

## Water Bowl

When the substrate and all the furnishings are in place, it is a good idea to put a water bowl into the enclosure. It is highly recommended that a water bowl filled with clean water should be available at all times. Both the leopard tortoise and the sulcata will use a water dish regularly and benefit greatly from doing so. When choosing a water bowl, be sure to select a dish that is

Large rocks and a potted plant make up the furnishings for this room-sized sulcata enclosure.

shallow enough for the tortoise to at least reach into, although it will usually climb all the way into the bowl if it is able to. The dish should be heavy enough that the tortoise does not knock the bowl around, spilling the water and making a mess. A good dish for this application is a flower pot saucer. If you go this route be sure to get a glazed dish for ease of cleaning, because tortoises are always getting into the water, and it is recommended that you keep the water as clean as possible. You might even want to consider keeping more than one dish on hand, trading them as needed. These particular dishes are inexpensive enough that this would not be cost prohibitive. These dishes can be found in the same places as where you would purchase the substrate.

## Heating and Lighting

With the enclosure set up with all the necessities as far as furnishings and water are concerned, there are a couple of final considerations with indoor housing, namely heating and lighting.

**Heat Sources** Tortoises need to select a range of temperatures to maintain their metabolism based on certain conditions. It is for this reason that a temperature gradient is recommended. This means you will provide your tortoise with a range of temperatures so that it can control its own body temperature. You will see that the tortoise will select different temperatures based on different needs. The tortoise will seek out warm temperatures when it is preparing to go out to forage and feed. It will then seek out a cooler temperature when it is bedding down for the evening.

The leopard tortoise and sulcata come from fairly warm climates, so a temperature range of 75 to 100°F (26.7 to 37.8°C) is a range that suits them. When you observe your tortoise,

## Heat Carefully

When using any supplemental heating, you always have to be careful to first make sure there is no potential that the heat source will injure the tortoise. The other consideration is to make sure there is no risk of a fire hazard. This applies to both indoor and outdoor enclosures. When using any electrical heat source, you should be sure it is rated for the amount of power you are using for that particular heat source. The use of surge protectors, ground-fault circuit interrupters, and thermostats is highly recommended. Also, be sure the equipment is rated for indoor or outdoor use, and it's never a good idea to use indoor-rated equipment outdoors.

Heat lamps are the most commonly used heat source for indoor tortoise enclosures.

you should see that it moves close to and then away from the heat source throughout the course of the day. If it is staying far away from the heat source all the time, the range is most likely too high. On the other hand, if it is spending all its time directly under or on top of the heat source the range is probably too low.

There are many sources of heat to choose from, but most are variations on two basic sources of heat: the overhead heat source and the underneath heat source. The most common overhead heat sources include the ceramic heat emitter and the incandescent lamp. The incandescent lamp produces heat as a byproduct of producing light, and the ceramic emitter gives off heat as a result of an electric current being passed through a resistive coil embedded in a ceramic core. The wattage of the lamp or emitter is going to determine the amount of heat produced. A higher wattage is going to produce a higher amount of heat. The amount of heat you are going to need is dependent on the ambient temperature of the area where the enclosure is placed. You will need a higher-wattage heat source if you live in a cooler climate or you keep the temperature of your home on the low side, and vice versa. The size of the enclosure will also affect the temperature; larger enclosures need higher-wattage heat sources. The only way to be certain as to how much heat you are going to need is to set up the enclosure and measure the temperature over the course of a given day—several days is even better.

The incandescent light is a good source of daytime heat because it provides a natural basking spot, but it is not a good heat source for the entire day, as it does not provide a day and night cycle. What many keepers do when heat is required through a 24-hour period is to use the ceramic emitter during the night and an incandescent lamp during the day to provide a day-night cycle indoors. This is easily accomplished by having two fixtures, one with a ceramic emitter and the other with an incandescent light. You can connect each of these to separate timers that you will set for whatever light cycle you choose.

The other method of providing heat is sometimes called an undertank heater. These are plastic mats with a resistive conductor embedded in plastic. They can vary in thickness from as thin as a sheet of paper to as thick as one inch (2.5 cm). These mats are usually placed under the enclosure. Undertank heaters should be used with caution, the reason being that they have a tendency to overheat if there is not enough air circulation. This problem can be overcome by making sure there is space between the mat and bottom of the enclosure. If the enclosure is on a flat surface it is a good idea to raise the enclosure using bricks or strips of wood on each end so the heat mat is not trapped between the two surfaces. Using a rheostat to adjust the power on an as-needed basis also helps in alleviating the potential problem of overheating. The heat mat can also be used as an overhead heat source in by attaching the mat to the ceiling of the tortoise's hiding place.

Regardless of what type of heat source you use it should be placed at one end of the enclosure to give you a maximum temperature gradient.

Leopards and sulcatas need exposure to ultraviolet light, from either natural sunlight or specialized light bulbs.

# The Great Outdoors

Outdoor enclosures are almost a necessity for keeping adult or near-adult sulcatas or leopard tortoises. Because of the size these tortoises attain, it is very difficult to maintain them indoors. The health benefits from natural sunlight and a well-planted yard, in addition to the space they have for grazing, cannot be disputed.

Another consideration when placing an overhead heat source is the height. Some heat sources get hot enough to burn flesh; care must be taken to place the heat source so that this does not become a risk. A good test to see if the height is sufficient is to hold your hand at the same level the top of the tortoise's shell is expected be. If it is too uncomfortable for you to keep your hand at that position, the heat source is probably too close or the power is too high.

**Lighting** Lighting has been mentioned only as a source of heat up until this point, but lighting also makes it pleasant to view the tortoise and provides daily cyclic cues for the tortoise to live by. There are special bulbs that provide ultraviolet B waves (UVB). This point will be covered in greater detail in the section on feeding. UVB bulbs do more than just provide light; they have the added benefit of providing the UVB tortoises need to metabolize calcium naturally. (At this point, the benefits of this type of lighting are unproven, but many tortoise keepers use them just to be on the safe side.)

Set up the lights on a 12-hour cycle, but you can vary the photoperiod if you want to simulate seasonal change. You can mount the lighting over the tortoise table by using 2- x 4-inch (5 x 10.2 cm) wood studs to form an arch over the table and attaching the lamps to that directly or hanging them from the arch. Another method of hanging the lighting is to use PVC tubing such as that used for plumbing. You can construct the arch using normal plumbing fittings for the angles and you can attach the arch to the table using pipe brackets. Be sure to use a tubing that is of sufficient size and thickness to support the light fixture. For fluorescent lighting you can use a single or double light strip mounted either directly to the arch or to the ceiling above the enclosure. In some instances you might have to suspend the light strip using chains in order to get the light closer to the tortoise.

A very common fixture for incandescent bulbs is an aluminum bell-shaped lamp. This can also be suspended from the arch. If this type of lamp is used, try to obtain lamps that have a high wattage rating and a ceramic fixture for the bulb for added safety. The ceramic fixture is especially important if you are using ceramic heat emitters. Be sure to mount any fixture securely for the safety of the tortoise and as an added precaution against any added fire hazard.

## Last Thoughts on Indoor Enclosures

So far this section has addressed accommodations that can house tortoises up to roughly 4 or 5 lbs (1.8-2.3 kg) in size. However, both the leopard and the sulcata do not stop growing at that size, presenting some unique problems for maintaining these tortoises indoors for any age past four or five years, although it is possible if you can provide them a separate room or a basement. If climate prevents you from maintaining these tortoises outdoors for most of the year or you cannot provide a separate building for them, you might want to reconsider keeping these species for any length of time. As mentioned earlier, sulcatas can be extremely destructive when they reach adult size.

# Outdoor Enclosures

As previously stated, outdoor housing is the preferred method for keeping tortoises. In the case of these African tortoises, it is the best way to maintain them given the potential size they reach as adults.

A chain-link fence enclosure will likely last the lifetime of your tortoise.

There are the same basic considerations for the outdoor enclosure as you have with an indoor enclosure, such as the size of the enclosure, substrate choice, etc. You will also have the added possibility of furnishing the enclosure with plants, which can be very difficult to do with an indoor enclosure.

## Size

The first and probably the most important consideration is going to be the size of the area that you are willing to or are able to provide. An area that is 6 feet by 10 feet (1.9 x 3 m) is sufficient to house a few young leopards or sulcatas, but you will quickly see that this would not suffice for the larger adult tortoises. Both species would need a recommended minimum area of 10 x 20 feet (3 x 6 m) for a pair of adults—and more space would be even better..

## Placement

When situating the enclosure, try to place the enclosure so it receives as much sunlight as possible. You do not want a location on the north side of a structure where the sun is blocked out most of the day. If the enclosure receives full sun throughout most of the day, you then have the option of adding plants or shelters to regulate the amount of sun the tortoises are exposed

# Fences

If you house your tortoise outdoors, you may want to fence in your yard. Having your enclosure in a fenced-in yard has several advantages. If your tortoise manages to escape from the enclosure, it will now have to get through the fence. This may give you the time you need to find your pet. Fencing helps keep out wildlife that could harm your tortoise. Additionally, it helps discourage anyone from coming in your yard and stealing or harming your tortoise. While most people wouldn't do that, there are those that would.

Wood treated for outdoor use is another material you can use to build a tortoise enclosure.

to. After all, it is the exposure to the sun that is a primary reason to house your tortoise outdoors.

## Materials

The task of constructing the barrier or fencing is the next project. There are several materials you can use, depending upon how much work, time, and money you wish to put into it. Some examples for fencing are treated wood, concrete, bricks, and chain link fencing. These are all suitable for both species of tortoises, but because of the sulcata's habit of burrowing it is not recommended that the chain-link fence be used for them unless the bottom 2 feet (61 cm) of the fencing is covered with a visual barrier and it extends at least a foot (30.5 cm) into the ground. This is not as much of a problem with the leopard tortoise.

**Bricks** Concrete blocks similar to cinder blocks or bricks are probably the best choice for these tortoises. They will probably provide you with the best security for the life of the tortoises. You will still need the bottom blocks to be buried at least one foot (30.5 cm) into the ground, as with any enclosure wall. You can also use a concrete footing, which can be made by digging a trench and then constructing a form that is filled with concrete. Any type of brick will make an attractive enclosure, but when using these materials it is necessary to properly cement the bricks in place, which requires a good deal of time and skill (and therefore money if you have to pay someone to do it). Once this is constructed, it is probably the most durable of all the enclosures. Before constructing any wall it is a good idea to dig a trench and fill a portion of that trench with a layer of gravel at least 1 foot (30.5 cm) deep. The wall will go on top of the gravel layer. In the case of the brick wall, the gravel provides a good foundation, and in the case of other types of enclosures it allows for good drainage, reducing moisture-caused rot.

**Chain-Link Fencing** A less expensive but equally as durable enclosure is the chain-link fence. There is a type of link fence that is called tennis court fencing because it is used for tennis courts or sports courts in general. What's special about this type of fencing is that it has a 1-inch (2.5-cm) mesh and is usually coated in plastic. The plastic comes in the colors of green or brown, so you can color-coordinate your yard. This type of enclosure is usually permanent in construction, as the corner posts are set in concrete for a good foundation for the fence. The fencing itself is probably going to have to be special-ordered from a fence outlet, but all the posts, rails, attaching hardware, and other materials can be easily found at any well-stocked home center. You will also need gravel and concrete mix to set the posts.

What is nice about chain-link fences is that they do not provide a solid barrier. From an esthetic point of view, it presents a more open and less enclosed look. The chain-link fence is also very durable and will last the life of the tortoise or group of tortoises. There is one

# Emergency!

When housing the sulcata or leopard tortoise outdoors, you should have a plan in the event there is an emergency that prevents keeping the tortoise outdoors for whatever reason.
Extreme weather events are the most likely reason, but this will vary with where you live. For this there should be temporary accommodations such as an indoor enclosure or an outdoor structure where the tortoise can be secured and kept safe. This should be thought out before you actually need it.

main disadvantage, and that is easily overcome. That disadvantage is that the tortoise can see through to the other side. Some animals will constantly try to get

The walls of your enclosure should extend beneath the ground, or your tortoise will be able to dig under them and escape.

through, as if they are in a glass enclosure. This situation can easily be remedied by using strips of plastic manufactured specifically for the purpose of preventing a clear view through the fence. The strips are woven through the links of the fence. If you cut the strips only to the height of the tortoise when it stands on its back legs, you preserve the open look of the enclosure while still restricting the tortoise's view.

**Other Materials** Pressure-treated wood is now another option for constructing a good strong fence. Today a copper-based chemical is used to preserve the wood, which is supposed to be less hazardous than the preservative chemicals of the past that were usually based on arsenic. The copper-treated wood is marked with an ACQ on the label. There are other materials you can use, which are only limited by your own imagination. With the previous listed examples

Hiding areas for outdoor tortoises can be simple or more elaborate. Here is one made from a dog house (bottom) and a custom-made one (top).

the possibilities you can come up with are really endless. The only points of interest that must be consistent no matter what material you use is that the material needs to be weather resistant. You also have to be certain the walls of the enclosure are buried deep enough to prevent the tortoise from digging out, especially with the sulcata. The final point in the construction of the outdoor enclosure is that the height of the enclosure does not have to be very high. The most practical height is high enough to step over yet not so low that the tortoise easily climbs over. A height of 24 to 36 inches (61 to 91.4 cm) above ground level is a good height for these tortoises.

## Soil and Grass

Once the enclosure is constructed, you should prepare the soil for growing plants before adding any structure to the enclosure. Ideally, you should have the soil tested for its nutrient content and how well it can support plants. This can usually be done at the county agricultural office for little to no charge. The office also usually provides suggestions for any deficiencies found in the soil. You then want to add mulch and manure, making sure to till the mixture in properly. It is also a good idea at this time to add any kind of soil conditioner, such as sand or gypsum, to break up any compacted soil and thereby provide better drainage.

With the enclosure constructed and the soil prepared, it is a good idea to establish grasses at this stage because these tortoises are very active grazers and trying to grow grass with the tortoises present would be very difficult. It is best to plant grasses that do well in your particular area. Your local lawn and garden shop will be your best source of information about the best grasses for your area. It is also a good idea to mix up the grass types to provide a good variety of feed for the tortoises.

## Hiding Place

Once the basic enclosure is set up the next step is to provide a hiding place to allow the tortoise to escape the elements while in the enclosure. The hide should be in an area that is well drained. Both the leopard and the sulcata come from relatively dry habitats. A humid enclosure is recommended, but a damp one could lead to health problems. If you don't have well-drained soil, you might consider removing the soil under the hide to a depth of roughly one foot, replacing the soil with sand or gravel and placing the hide on top of that. Once that is done, a bed of hay or some other soft substrate would be a good finishing touch for the inside of the hide.

Sulcatas dig large burrows. Be careful when maintaining the enclosure; you could easily fall into one of your pet's burrows.

The hide can consist of something as simple as a wooden or plastic box to something as complex as a small house or shed. The decision on what type of hide you use will depend mostly on the average temperature the tortoise will encounter.

In warmer climates where the evening temperatures do not get below 75°F (23.9°C), a hide such as a wooden box will work just fine. In climates that experience colder temperatures, the hide will need to be more elaborate and heated.

The entrance to the hide should be covered with either cloth or plastic sheeting as added protection against the elements. This also helps retain heat when a supplemental heat source is used. Supplemental heating is recommended for sulcatas and leopards whenever the temperature drops below 75°F (23.9°C), although these two species can normally withstand temperatures as low as 50°F (10°C) provided they can warm up sufficiently during the day time. Provide supplemental heating in the same manner as in the indoor enclosure, but taking extreme caution to make sure the heat source and the power to the heat source are well protected from the weather. It is also a good idea to provide a ground fault interrupt in the power circuit to prevent electrocution of the tortoise and yourself. Place the heat source toward the rear of the hide for the best efficiency.

Some common heat sources that are used for outdoor enclosures are heat mats and ceramic heat emitters. The emitters are small enough to fit into most hides, but they are inefficient in larger hide boxes unless the hide is well insulated. It is suggested that the ceramic heater be installed in a ceramic fixture mounted in such a manner that the tortoise cannot hit it or be burned by the heat source. It can be attached to the ceiling of the hide or even mounted on the wall.

For the larger hide areas, a heat mat or pig blanket is recommended. Pig blankets are plastic mats intended to provide a warm area to farm animals. They are manufactured to be weatherproof, but the connection for the power to the mat is not, so caution must be taken

# Plants

**Which plants you use for your tortoise enclosure will depend on your climate and what is available at your local gardening stores. In most places, there will be hundreds you can choose from. The following list provides only a few suggestions.**

| | |
|---|---|
| **Ficus** | **Mulberry** |
| **Grape** | **Rose** |
| **Hibiscus** | **Rose of Sharon** |
| **Lavender** | **Waxleaf** |

Sulcata feeding on grape vines planted to hang over into its enclosure.

to cover the connection so that it is waterproof. These heat mats come in many sizes and can be purchased at many pet stores or animal feed stores. They can also be ordered online. The mat itself should not be totally covered. This will not only increase the risk of fire but also might reduce the life of the mat.

Another safety precaution that you should take regardless of the heat source is the use of a thermostat and/or timer. With a thermostat you can set the heat source to come on when the outside temperatures dip below a comfortable level. If the heat source is allowed to produce heat full time, there is a chance that the tortoise can overheat (not to mention that it is a waste of energy and money to have the heat on during the time when it is unnecessary). Adding foam insulation to the inside of the hide box can further reduce the cost of heating, but the foam needs to be sandwiched between the wall and some form of protection such as 1/2- to 3/4- inch (1.3 to 1.9 cm) plywood for protection from the sharp and strong arms of a sulcata.

## Water

The introduction of water cannot be over-emphasized. Even in an outdoor enclosure that gets watered on a regular basis the placement of a water bowl or dish is highly recommended. As with the indoor enclosure, a glazed flower pot saucer makes a great water dish. You can sink the dish into the ground so the lip is about a quarter inch (0.6 cm) above ground level. A 12-inch (30.5-cm)-diameter dish would be considered a minimal size for the outdoor enclosure. The water should be changed daily. This task is made easier by using the spray blast from a water hose to remove the old water and decreasing the pressure to refill the dish. This makes removing the dish unnecessary..

When providing water for the outdoor pen you are not limited to the use of a dish. You can also make a concrete water catch in the shape of a pond or stream. Be sure to properly seal the concrete to prevent the leaching of any chemicals that are found in concrete and also to prevent the concrete from becoming saturated and crumbling. These types of water dispensers can look great in an outdoor enclosure and are no harder to service than the ceramic dish.

## Furnishings

Before you add the plants and tortoises, you may want to add rocks and logs. These items are important in that they seem to make the enclosure bigger by breaking up the open space. In the instance of a single tortoise this provides it with something to occupy it by forcing it to go around, over, and through the structure. If you have more than one tortoise, the structures also provide a visual barrier in the event that there is any aggression between the tortoises. The visual barriers will allow the line of sight to be broken in a pursuing tortoise. You will quickly see that a tortoise is easily distracted, so when the line of sight is broken the tortoise that is the aggressor or pursuer usually gives up pursuit. When placing these visual barriers, you want to use up as little actual floor space as possible. The idea is to provide barriers that the tortoise can use, such as rocks and logs that are leaned and raised against another structure. Be careful to make sure any raised structure is securely in place so there is no danger of the object's

falling and crushing any of the inhabitants of the enclosure. Also be careful that the tortoise cannot use an object to climb over the walls of the enclosure.

## Plants

At this point you can choose to add plants or not. Adding plants gives you that instant gratification that the enclosure is complete. If you choose not to add plants, you will see that over time the local vegetation will find its way into the enclosure. This is sometimes the better way to go, because the first plants that usually colonize a vacant piece of land are usually broadleaf weeds and grasses. These can serve as good forage material for the tortoise.

Observe your tortoise closely in its new home to see whether there is anything that needs to be added or improved.

To actually compile a list of the types of plants you could use to add to the enclosure would fill a large book in itself, considering all the regional differences that exist throughout the areas in which leopard tortoises and sulcatas occur and are kept as pets. It is for this reason the discussion on the plants you can use will be presented in general terms.

When providing plants in the enclosure, try to keep in mind that the plants are going to grow. Try to envision what the plants will look like in a year from the time you planted them. The point is that you want to provide enough space for the plants to grow into. As mentioned earlier, grasses and weeds are going to establish themselves, so the plants you want to provide are those that are going to provide shade or cover. Plants such as hedges, small bushes, and even some small trees are good for this because they are slow growers for the most part. If you treat them as if they were miniature trees or bonsai and keep them trimmed to a small size, they can become a very pleasant addition to the enclosure as well as being a functional part of the contained ecosystem.

When selecting the plants for the enclosure, it is good practice to select plants that are not toxic to animals. This is not a critical point, since there are many plants that are toxic to mammals but not toxic to reptiles. Also, tortoises seem to know what they can and cannot eat provided that they are not starved and do have a choice. For your own peace of mind and to be on the safe side, refrain from using any plants that may be toxic. To find out whether a plant is toxic or not, you can consult the nursery where you bought the plants. You can also inquire about the plants at the biology department at your local museum of natural history or any major college or university. Searching through the many lists on the Internet to find any plants in question usually yields very good

results. This task of finding out about a plant is made much simpler if you know the scientific name of the plant you purchase. Many times the toxicity of a plant is listed in the written information provided about the care of that plant by the seller.

When selecting plants, also try to obtain plants that might be useful for more than just providing shade and cover. Selecting plants that you know to be edible is a good practice. There are many books available that list edible plants, including trees and shrubs. More on this will be discussed in the section on feeding and nutrition.

## Adding the Tortoise

With the enclosure finished and ready for occupancy, you can place the tortoise within. It is always a good idea to watch the tortoise very carefully for the first few weeks. It is the tortoise that will tell you where the shortcomings of the enclosure are, and there are always

Tortoises kept outdoors must have access to shaded areas, so they can get out of the sun if they feel too warm.

little and not so little things that you will need to adjust. The main things to look for are points of escape and points of potential injury. These usually show up pretty quickly with a sulcata, considering how active this tortoise is. Leopard tortoises, on the other hand, are usually pretty calm tortoises, so this is not so much of a problem with this species. Another important point is to make sure you see the tortoise use the water dish. You might have to show the tortoise where the water dish is a few times. Also watch to see whether the tortoise is using the enclosure or hide that is provided, and try to set it up so that it does use it. Sulcatas are pretty good about using an enclosure, and they should be encouraged to do so because if they do not find a comfortable place to rest at night they will dig a burrow of their own. For a larger sulcata, this can easily be as large as 2 feet (61 cm) in diameter and well over 15 feet (4.6 m) long. If you're not careful you can easily lose a small child or the family pet in such a hole. Also, if there is inadequate drainage the tortoise can easily drown in its own burrow. It is for these reasons that the digging of its own burrow should be discouraged in the case of a sulcata. Leopard tortoises are not active diggers for the most part, but they are notorious for not using provided houses. This can be a problem if they are maintained outdoors in areas where a heated house is required. It is important to make sure the leopard is placed in the heated house on a nightly basis if it does not do this on its own. Once the breaking-in period for the outdoor enclosure is complete, the enclosure can last for many years without any care at all if planned and constructed properly.

# Chapter 4

# Feeding and Nutrition

T he most basic items in terms of nutrition for your tortoise are food and water. This seems simple and obvious at first glance, but the apparent simplicity of the idea is misleading: food and water will be of no use if the tortoise cannot metabolize the material. This is mentioned here because it is a very important point; many keepers take it for granted that if they just provide food and water their tortoises will be taken care of nutritionally, and that simply is not true.

## The Natural Diet

It is common practice when keeping tortoises in captivity to try to provide as natural a diet as possible. This is more difficult than it sounds, because the only way you are going to know exactly what your species eats in the wild is to observe many tortoises over the entire range over many years. There will be differences among different populations and even between different individuals. Available food types will vary based on regional and seasonal differences. Once you have this sorted out you now have to obtain the very food the tortoises consume —difficult with sulcatas and leopards because of the native region. As you can imagine this would be a monumental task as well as unrealistic to undertake. If you look at where wild tortoises come from, you will see that they have an immense variety of plants, insects, and other items to choose from. Again, these choices will vary on a seasonal and regional basis.

In nature, both the sulcata and the leopard tortoise are primarily grazers and browsers. They are known to consume broadleaf weeds in addition to succulents and other plant materials, including native fruits, tree branches, and even the bark of woody plants. They will also consume insects and carrion on a relatively frequent basis. As opportunistic feeders in a harsh environment, both of these tortoises will consume almost any material that could possibly help sustain them. This point is especially relevant when considering the sulcata.

Tortoises kept outdoors will forage for much of their own food, grazing on grass and weeds.

## A Lot Left to Learn

Much of the available nutritional information is based on models created for mammals. While this is the only starting point we have, it does not take into account that tortoises are ectothermic. There have been only limited studies of reptile nutrition, and even fewer specifically of tortoise nutrition.

## The Importance of Variety

What keepers do to overcome the impossibility of providing a truly natural diet is to provide a substitute diet. Normally keepers offer a diet that has been successfully used on captive tortoises by others in years past. Many of the currently recommended diets were originally based on limited observations and studies of similar tortoises with similar needs. In the end, over the years, the main diet of these animals in captivity is ultimately a result of trial and error.

The way to provide the best nutritional balance in captivity is to provide a variety, as much of a variety as possible. Many tortoise keepers make the mistake of focusing on specific components. If you focus on any one specific component, the most likely result is an overage in that component or a deficiency in another component. This is mentioned because commonly there is an overemphasis on individual components (such as feeding a low-protein, high-fiber diet) where tortoises are concerned. This seems to be an overreaction to the old practice of feeding dog and cat food to the family pet tortoise. Feeding dog or cat food to these tortoises usually does lead to a severely deformed unhealthy tortoise. Through the years, we have discovered that this is not a good diet for these particular tortoises. Their digestive system is not set up to process the fat and animal protein that dog and cat foods contain. They are primarily vegetarian, eating mostly grasses and weeds.

**The Fuzzy Tortoise**

You can think of a tortoise as a bunny with a shell. Rabbits are one of the hindgut fermenters, a classification based on how they digest their food. This means that the food, which is usually high in fiber, is broken down by fermentation in the hindgut and not the stomach for the most part. They have very much the same feeding habits and similar digestive process as a tortoise, but the tortoise has the added complication of being dependent on its environment to provide the heat to process its food.

## Digestive System

We know that tortoises have a type of digestive system called hindgut fermentation. Their digestive tracts are similar to those of rabbits and horses. The stomach is very crude, and not much digestion actually takes place there. Most of the digestion process takes place in the large intestine with the aid of aerobic bacteria. A good portion of digestion takes place in

Sulcata and leopard tortoises eat almost constantly during their active periods.

this modified large intestine, so a good amount of food is wasted because the next step for the food is to be evacuated. This is important because the tortoises' digestive system has evolved to be very efficient with what little nutrients it extracts.

These tortoises are eating constantly when they are active. This stands to reason, as the foods they are eating are for the most part so nutrient-poor that the tortoises have to eat almost constantly to obtain sufficient nutrition to survive, grow, and reproduce. Most tortoises, including the sulcata and leopard tortoise, are most likely not exclusively hindgut fermenters. Nutrients seem to be taken in by the stomach and small intestine also, which enables the tortoises to make some use of animal protein. Looking back to where these animals are found in nature, you can see how they have adapted to survive in mostly harsh environments. This point will become more important when we first understand the major components of nutrition. .

## Major Nutrients

While there are many important nutrients, the major ones that concern tortoise keepers are protein, fiber, minerals, and vitamins. If you look at protein, fiber, minerals, and vitamins individually you might be able to get a better understanding of how they fit together. Keep in mind that there are other components, but these four are the major components that are used by the tortoise, so they deserve particular attention. If these components are in balance the others components will fall into place if you provide a varied diet.

## Protein

Protein is the most important component of nutrition because it is the major physical building block of all life. In simple terms, protein is made up of a fixed number of specific chemicals called amino acids. The sequence in which the amino acids fit together and the shape of the structure that is formed by the combinations of these acids determines the type of protein. Proteins not only form structural building blocks but also provide specific functions in the internal processes within all living things.

Protein seems to be the least understood nutrient as far as tortoises are concerned. This leads to many misconceptions. Excess protein is blamed on many physical problems in the development of tortoises, including the malformation of the carapace called pyramiding. The problem with this line of thought is that it is really not known with any certainty that protein is the actual culprit, because it is not known how much protein is required and how that protein is processed in tortoises.

There is a common belief that too much protein is bad. This could be true; too much of any one thing is bad because it leads to an imbalance or deficiency of the other nutritional components. The problem with this line of thought is that when we think of protein in tortoise nutrition we really do not know what "too much" is. The best way to overcome this hurdle is to provide as much variety as possible and try not to fixate on any one single item.

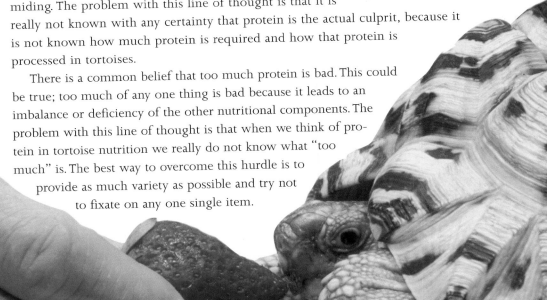

Sulcatas and leopards are primarily herbivorous; feed your tortoise very little animal matter.

Protein is a very necessary component of nutrition for the proper development of any living creature, but as far as tortoise nutrition goes we really don't know the actual requirements.

Sulcata and leopard tortoises are herbivores for the most part. The main source of protein should be from plant material. As was mentioned earlier, these animals are hindgut fermenters, so the amount of protein that they actually obtain from their natural forage is going to be minimal by design of their digestive tract. The actual protein content of any plant should not be a concern if the plant is part of a varied diet. Animal protein should not be fed, because most animal protein is usually associated with fat. Some herpetologists believe that the fat and not the protein is the real problem (although the animal protein itself could very well be the problem). This is yet another controversial topic for which there is very little hard data. The safest course for your tortoise is to focus on plant material as the primary source of protein and make certain to offer as much variety as possible. If you notice that the tortoise does consume the occasional insect or animal matter, there should be no cause for alarm as long as such foods do not become a staple of the tortoise's diet.

## Fiber

The next important component in tortoise nutrition is fiber. Fiber is considered the indigestible plant material that is consumed by the tortoise. Fiber serves the function of retaining moisture and aiding in digestion. In hindgut fermenters, this is also the case and

## Cultivating Cactus

Pear cactus, *Opuntia* sp., is a calcium-rich plant and a good addition to your tortoise's diet. It can be found in well-stocked supermarkets and specialty grocery stores, as well as in the arid areas of North America. You can also grow it yourself, as this cactus is easily propagated. Begin by cutting a pad along the seam at the bottom of the pad where it attaches to the main plant. Allow the cut to dry out for a day or two, and then plant the pad in a 1- to 1- ratio of a soil and sand mixture. Plant the pad with the cut end just below the surface. Water regularly but allow the surface to dry between waterings. In a few months, you will have a good supply of cactus to feed your tortoises—and yourself.

Variety is the key to a healthy diet for these tortoises. However, very moist foods should be fed sparingly.

more so because the fiber is digested with the aid of beneficial bacteria that live in the hindgut. This actually adds to the other components of nutrition because the fiber is broken down into its component nutrients.

It is commonly believed that these tortoises need a high-fiber and low-protein diet. In actuality you want to feed a balanced diet that has the correct ratio of all the required nutrients and not focus on any one particular nutrient But since you really can't tell the actual composition of what you are feeding, once again variety of the diet becomes the key to overcoming the unknowns. There are so many unknowns that the only way we can get around them is to provide as much choice to the tortoise as possible. Fiber or roughage is also reported to aid in keeping the parasite load down in tortoises in the wild. If you are maintaining your tortoise or tortoises outdoors, this is something that should be considered. No matter how diligent you are in maintaining a parasite-free area, your tortoise is likely to pick up internal parasites, and roughage will usually help to keep the parasite load to a minimum.

# Check the Temperature

**The first warning sign that something is wrong with any tortoise is usually the refusal of food. Your first response to this warning sign is to check the temperature range in the tortoise enclosure. If the tortoise is too cool or even too hot it will refuse food. Adjusting the range up or down as needed usually brings the tortoise back to its normal feeding pattern.**

## Vitamins

Vitamins are the next important component in nutrition. Vitamins are minute components that are essential in aiding the normal biological processes in the body but are not produced by the body. This might sound a bit vague, and it is. What we know about vitamins in mammals is that they are required, and they are not produced by the body. Any deficiency in these vitamins will lead to a deficiency disease. If you are supplementing certain vitamins in certain forms it can also lead to a poisoning situation. This sounds simple, but it only demonstrates again how little is actually known about vitamins in living organisms and their interactions.

In mammals we know that vitamins are required in a specific ratio based again on biological models. We also know that different species require different vitamins in different ratios. We've got a clue as to what is required in tortoises, but it is once again based on mammalian models, which has the major flaw of not taking into account the thermal requirement for reptiles and is sure to produce a large margin of error. In the end, what this means is that we really don't know for sure what the vitamin requirements for tortoises are.

There are many vitamin supplements available. The only way to be certain that any of them are of any good is to try them and observe the results you obtain with your tortoise under the conditions you are providing. It is recommended that you start with those vitamins that have been around the longest time and have a noteworthy reputation among tortoise keepers. It is also recommended that you use a vitamin that has withstood the test of time. Talk to other keepers and look at the results that they have achieved. If you are feeding the recommended varied diet there should be little need for vitamin supplements, but use a vitamin supplement once a week or so to be on the safe side. Over time, if you see you are obtaining the results you are looking for with only the foods you are feeding, you can omit the supplemental vitamins altogether.

## Minerals

The final major component of nutrition to consider for your tortoise is minerals. Minerals are basic elements that make up a very small portion of the chemical composition of the body, but they are extremely important in providing structural material, providing regulatory mechanisms for the normal metabolic processes, and for the basic functions of life. Two of the most important minerals in tortoises are calcium and phosphorus. Both of these minerals are of equal importance because it is the interaction of these two minerals that regulates each of them. If you focus on one and not the other you are almost certain to lead to an imbalance that in turn is most likely to lead to health problems. There are a large number of other important minerals, including sodium, potassium, iron, and others, but providing a var-

Pear cactus makes a nutritious food for tortoises and is fairly easy to grow.

ied diet usually supplies your tortoise with an adequate supply of these nutrients.

The comments about supplementation made in the vitamin section apply to minerals as well. When feeding a wide variety of different foods, there will be little need for mineral supplementation, but you should add a bit of powdered supplement weekly to be on the safe side. The human multivitamin/multimineral Centrum is widely recommended by tortoise keepers. It isn't difficult to grind the tablets into a powder and sprinkle it over the tortoise's food.

**Calcium** It was suggested earlier in this text that supplemental vitamins and minerals should be used sparingly. There is one exception to this: calcium. Calcium is probably the single most important mineral in all of tortoise nutrition. This is not to say that all the other components are not important, but calcium seems to be the most utilized and the most problematic in tortoises. The calcium ion is necessary for many bodily functions, including muscle contractions, nerve impulses, bone and shell structure, and activation of enzymes, among other things. This is the one mineral that is recommended for supplementation at every feeding.

The most easily attainable and usable form of calcium is calcium carbonate. This form—if used in conjunction with natural sunlight—is very difficult to overdose, which is why it is recommended. It would appear that tortoises in general are very susceptible to bone and shell deformities. The body is designed to maintain in the blood a specific level of calcium that provides for all the bodily functions involved with the mineral. When this level drops, the thyroid gland releases one hormone that stimulates a release of calcium from the bone while also increasing calcium retention by the kidney and calcium uptake by the intestines (the latter requires vitamin D3). When all is in balance, the thyroid gland releases a different

## The More Variety, the Better

**Because there are so many options for providing different forms of nutrition, there is no reason why a keeper cannot easily provide a varied diet. When a good variety is provided, most if not all the nutritional needs of your tortoise are easily met. Coupled with the proper environment, a good variety of foods should give you a well-developed tortoise with little or no problems.**

hormone that signals the kidney and intestine to reduce calcium uptake and at the same time encourages the deposition of calcium in the bone.

This is one reason why hydration is critical to the health of these tortoises. If the kidneys are stressed or functioning poorly, it will affect calcium metabolism. Since these animals come from very dry areas, their hydration needs are often taken for granted. It is sometimes assumed that these tortoises obtain adequate hydration from the foods they consume. In the wild this might be the case because the tortoises have some control of water loss through the selection of their microhabitat. In captivity, they are completely dependent on you for their hydration needs.

Many tortoise breeders recommend adding supplemental calcium to the diet at almost every feeding.

Hatchlings are especially vulnerable to dehydration and its effects on calcium metabolism. It is believed that hatchlings, because of their small size, dehydrate very quickly. There have been numerous reports of hatchlings failing to thrive and also having a soft shell. It is now suspected that the actual cause of this failure to thrive is kidney failure due to dehydration, which in turn affects bone and shell development. This point cannot be stressed enough, and if more keepers monitor hydration with close attention it will probably lead to the survival of many more juvenile tortoises.

One of the easiest sources of calcium to obtain is calcium carbonate. This can be found in the form of a powder or as a solid in the form of cuttlebone. Cuttlebone is the internal skeleton of a cuttlefish, a squid-like creature. It has been used as a calcium supplement for birds for many years. The cuttlebone can be fed whole or ground up into a powder. When feeding only calcium carbonate, it is important to remember that the tortoise's body does not process the calcium without vitamin D3. This can be obtained as a supplement, or the body can produce the D3 in the skin when exposed to natural sunlight or any source of ultraviolet B lighting. By using calcium carbonate and natural sunlight, you allow the body to regulate the calcium naturally. When D3 is used as a supplement there is the added risk of overdosing with calcium, which can lead to having calcium deposited in the tissues and joints of the tortoise.

While this is definitely a major simplification of the general nutritional requirements of these two species, it should give you an idea of what is actually known about their needs and what you are going to have to provide. As you can see, there is a great deal of guesswork involved in providing an adequate and nutritious diet for your tortoise. After the environmental facilities, this area is where most, if not all, keepers have the greatest difficulty. It is also the area where there is the greatest amount of confusion and controversy among tortoise keepers. In the rest of this chapter, some of the more troublesome points will be addressed so that your part of the guesswork can be reduced to a minimum.

## Pet Diet

In the wild, sulcatas and leopards are mainly grazers, but they supplement that grazing material when the opportunity presents itself. Which plants the tortoises eat depends on the home range of the individual and the season of the year. Sulcatas have adapted to some very harsh environments, and as such they have adapted to eat almost anything. This does not mean that you should feed just about anything to a sulcata, because nine times out of ten what you feed them, they will eat. The leopard tortoise tends to be a little more selective. In either case it is up to you to regulate what is available to the tortoise.

**Another Hydration Issue**

Proper hydration is critical to successfully keeping tortoises as pets. This point seems to be most important with sulcata tortoises, because inadequate hydration can cause them to form kidney or bladder stones. This problem is not as prevalent in leopard tortoises, although they need adequate hydration as well.

### Plants from Yards and Fields

If you are lucky enough to maintain your tortoise outdoors (even for just part of the year), feeding becomes easier because the tortoise will be able to forage and choose what it wishes to eat in an adequately planted enclosure. This gives you the opportunity to see which plants the tortoise keys onto. It is during the time the tortoise is outdoors that you will gather the most valuable

Dark leafy greens can make up a large percentage of your tortoise's diet.

information if you take notice of the tortoise's behavior.

Always try to let the tortoise tell you what it needs or what it likes. Watch the plants your turtle consumes. Unless the tortoise is starving it is only going to consume the plants that are appealing to it. From this you can get an idea of what exactly to feed your tortoise if you have seasons that prevent you from letting the tortoise forage outdoors all year. As an example, if you notice your tortoise feeding on broad leafy greens you can easily assume you will have no trouble providing dark leafy greens that you can find in any produce section of the food market. On the other hand, if the tortoise is feeding mainly on grasses you can either cut and dry your own supply of grasses or find at a local feed store a hay similar to the grass it has been feeding on. You can also find other foods at a pet supply outlet on the Internet.

Although sulcatas and leopards are grazers for the most part, they will also consume broad leafy greens. This can include all those nasty weeds that come up in your lawn. Lawns, open fields, empty lots, school grounds, and city parks are all excellent hunting grounds for finding  a good variety natural fare for your tortoise (just check to make sure these places aren't being sprayed with pesticides or fertilizers). Lawn clippings can also be

# Plant Cautions

**Not every plant that tortoises consume is safely edible by mammals. What that means is that if a plant is poisonous to you it is not necessarily poisonous to the tortoise. With that said, you should not allow your tortoise to consume plants that you know to be poisonous, but at the same time you can trust your tortoise to know what it can and cannot consume— within reason. If the tortoise is not starving, it will pass on the plants it does not like and move on to the ones it does. Eliminate obviously poisonous plants from the enclosure, but don't fret over each and every species of weed that springs up.**

used to supplement the feeding of these tortoises. You can even grow your own weeds if you so choose. There are many companies that sell seeds for many of the weeds that are acceptable food for your tortoise. The list of the available plants that you can feed is virtually endless, but your best source of specific information is going to be a book on the local edible plants of your area.

The sulcata and leopard will also readily consume the commonly available weeds such as plantain, milk thistle, dandelions, and the like. Focus on any broad leafy green that is seasonal. These are usually the plants that pop up after a rain and die off after a few months. The leaves are usually very thin. They are the most abundant in the spring, but as you move closer geographically to the equator the winter becomes the prominent season for these plants. Again, keep in mind that your tortoise is usually not choosy, and there are not many plants that emerge in the spring that are harmful. If you have any question as to whether a plant is suitable or not, your local museum or plant nursery is usually a good source to confirm any suspicions you might have. Again your tortoise is going to be your key indicator. It should tell you what is good for it or not. As stated earlier, if the tortoise is not starving it will usually not consume any plant that is bad for it. If the tortoise does take a bite of a plant that you are not sure of and you see the tortoise spit it out, it is usually a good idea to remove the remainder of the plant and any similar plants in the area just to be on the safe side. Keep in mind that this is something that you do not have to be overly careful about. These animals do seem to know

Usually considered a weed, dandelions are highly nutritious and make a good addition to your tortoises's diet.

what they can and can't eat.

When you are collecting plants away from your own property, it is a good idea to know the practice of the groundskeepers of the areas you are collecting from. You want to be relatively certain that pesticides or any other chemicals have not been used. Schools and public parks are usually a safe bet because of the presence of children, but it is also a good idea to monitor an area that you are interested in collecting from to see whether chemicals or any evidence of chemicals is being used. Collecting plants from the roadside is usually not a good idea because of the emissions from automobiles that are sure to not only settle on the plants but are also as sure to be absorbed by the plants. Sulcatas and leopards will also browse on the leaves of trees and bushes such as mulberry, hibiscus, ficus, forsythia, rose, and grape vines to name a few.

Most of the previously mentioned plants usually give rise to flowers, fruits, and berries. These items can be fed also. If you do feed fruits, you should be careful to feed them sparingly. These tortoises have adapted to feed on relatively dry items, so high-moisture items should be avoided. Fruits with a low moisture content, such as apples, pears, berries, and the like are acceptable. Many of these items can be dehydrated and stored during the periods that they are not available. The plant can be rehydrated or fed dry on an as-needed basis. Be

Many common garden plants are good foods for tortoises. Squash (in the foreground) produces edible leaves, flowers, and fruit.

# Mmm...Grass

**Some suggested grasses that have successfully been used for providing graze for the sulcata and leopard tortoise are Bermuda grass, St. Augustine, centipede grass, fescue, and orchard grass. There are many more grasses that can be used, because it does not appear that these tortoises really have a preference when it comes to grazing. The key is always to provide as much variety as possible.**

careful to keep it dry to avoid spoilage. If the material gets moldy, it can make your tortoise sick.

## Plants From the Grocery Store

In certain instances, it may not be possible to provide a weed- and grass-based diet, and there is nothing wrong with this. The basic rule of providing as much variety as possible still stands. If you do turn to the greens that you find in the produce section of the grocery store, try to focus on the dark leafy greens. If you are providing as much variety as possible, there are no limits for the most part. The only caution is to be careful not to over-use beans and related plants, if you use them at all. These have been implicated in some nutritional disorders when fed in excess. Some of the more commonly used store-bought produce items are lettuces, kale, escarole, endive, romaine, collard greens, mustard greens, spinach, and shredded carrots. Almost everything else in the produce department can be fed as part of a highly varied diet. The only suggestions are to mix it up as much as possible and, where the lettuces are concerned, try to select the darkest green varieties. Fruits such as apples, pears, and berries can also be fed to add to the variety, but high-moisture fruits such as melons should be avoided.

## Commercial Tortoise Foods

As the hobby of keeping tortoises grows more and more, commercial products made just for tortoises are making their way onto the market. There are many vita-

There are some good commercial tortoise diets available. Use them to increase variety in your tortoise's diet.

This leopard tortoise helps himself to some cactus.

min/mineral supplements and even packaged foods. Many of these items are of questionable value. Those of questionable value usually come and go fairly quickly, but there are also some products that have been around for some time and they do make good nutrition easier and healthier for the present-day pet tortoise.

There are several packaged foods that seem to be very well formulated and also appear to be beneficial. These package foods are yet another route you can choose to increase the variety you can provide. When selecting one of these foods, it is always a good suggestion to speak to as many keepers as you can that have used the food or are using it. There is one caution when using some of the grain-based foods. Some seem to be very nutritious. What this means is that when they are fed to sulcatas and leopard tortoises in large amounts it can lead to very rapid growth. Whether this is a good or bad thing is yet another topic of much debate, but it can be controlled if desired by reducing the amount of this type of food you offer. What is also interesting with some of these foods is that while the growth is rapid, it is very smooth and even, as you would expect from a tortoise that has been feeding in the wild. If any of these foods are used in feeding these tortoises, limit it to once or twice a week.

## How Much and How Often

Once you know what to feed your tortoise, you might wonder how much and how often the tortoise should be fed. In nature, when the tortoise is active it is usually feeding, but if you remember from the notes in the natural history section they are not active very often in their native harsh environment. Also, the foods they are feeding on are usually very nutrient poor. For this reason, development is slow and overfeeding is not a concern. In captivity, your tortoise is given ideal conditions, so its feeding schedule is going to be quite different from what you would expect to find in nature. If you feed a limited quantity, you can feed every day to stimulate activity. If you are feeding mostly fibrous plants, there should be no concern about overfeeding, with few exceptions. The only time overfeeding may become a problem is if you are feeding a very rich or nutritious diet. In that situation you would want to limit the quantity as you would with manufactured foods. You can also supplement these foods with a high-fiber component such as hay or grass for better balance. Packages of these hays used as rabbit and small-animal foods are found in most pet stores, and these prepackaged hays are perfectly acceptable for tortoises.

You should notice that your tortoise is most active in the morning and in the late afternoons. These are usually good times to feed to be sure the tortoise has the opportunity to eat. It is also a good idea to scatter or hide the food to encourage activity and browsing. You

# Recycling

You might see your sulcata or leopard tortoise consume its own feces. This is very common with the sulcata, although leopards will do the same thing on occasion. While this might be an unpleasant sight, it is actually thought to be an important part of tortoise nutrition. These tortoises are hindgut fermenters, so many nutrients are not absorbed. It is suspected that this practice of consuming its own feces, called coprophagy, is a means of reducing the waste of available nutrients. This is similar to running the food through the digestive process a second time to absorb those nutrients made available when the material was broken down in the hindgut fermentation process the first time around.

should not be too concerned if your tortoise ingests a little substrate with its food as long as the substrate does not have any sharp edges such as splinters or the tortoise does not ingest the substrate directly as if it were food. If you are using a grass or hay substrate this is not a concern at all. Leaving the remains of leafy greens is not a problem as long as the material does not stay wet and rot. The tortoises seem to actually enjoy foraging on dried greens. All other uneaten food should be removed once the tortoise has retired for the day.

## Last Thoughts

In closing on the topic of nutrition, you have to remember that because the tortoise is so dependent on its environment, particularly temperature, the rates of growth and the type of development are going to vary from tortoise to tortoise. Adding to this the variance that you have among individual tortoises in their behavior, there is a certainty that most people will get varying results. If you do see a result in the development that you do not like, first look at the environmental conditions and then consider the diet.

While calcium is probably the most challenging and obvious component in the quest for proper nutrition in tortoises, it is not the only topic of focus. There are many other deficiencies that come up but seem to be caused by a very simple problem: many keepers tend to feed a very limited range of foods. Some keepers also feed inappropriate foods. These are two very simple problems to overcome. It is now well known that if keepers provide an adequate variety, nutritional deficiencies are virtually eliminated. This can be easy if you keep an open mind. All plant material is fair game for a tortoise's diet.

# Chapter 5

# Breeding and Reproduction

**T**he best evidence that could be provided as an indication that your tortoises are properly cared for is provided when the tortoises complete the life cycle and breed in your care. This usually indicates that the tortoises are healthy and the environment that has been provided is acceptable to them.

A sulcata tortoise will be able to breed at a size of approximately 15 inches (38.1 cm).

There are many different factors that need to come together to provide any success in reaching the goal of breeding your tortoises. The most important factor is the provision of the proper environment matched with a good diet to ensure that the animals are in good health. The next factor is to be certain that you have a male and a female and they are of breeding size. Hopefully, this pair will be compatible. With any luck, they will breed and with a little more luck they will produce eggs, and still with a little more luck the eggs will be fertile and with just a little bit more luck the eggs will hatch to give you some nice healthy offspring. So you see, there is a great deal of luck involved even if everything falls into place. Here we'll discuss certain things you can do to increase your chances of success.

## Breeding Age and Size

Most keepers will start off with captive-bred tortoises. This increases the chances of successful breeding, because you are not dealing with an animal that is fixated on natural cues to stimulate breeding. The only disadvantage is that you have to raise the tortoise from hatchling to adult, and that will take time. This can be as little as four years up to 20 years for both of these species. When you take the time to raise your tortoise from hatchling to breeding size, the feeling of accomplishment is so much greater when you complete the cycle and produce more hatchlings.

With leopard and sulcata tortoises, the time when they first can breed is more of a factor of size than of age. In other words, size more than age determines whether the tortoise can reproduce or not. These tortoises can reach breeding size in as little as four years if you provide an ideal mix of diet and environment in addition to keeping that mix constant. (We still don't know whether an accelerated growth rate has any detrimental effects on the long-term health of tortoises.) Normally, most tortoises will go through seasonal cycles of rapid growth and slower growth, depending on the environmental conditions. This will slow the overall growth rate. With this in mind, you can expect your tortoise to reach breeding size in about ten years. During that time, you can set up a cycle that your tortoise will hopefully use for its own breeding cues. A breeding-size female sulcata tortoise is approximately 15 inches (38.1 cm) SCL. The male is mature at a length of about the same size. Leopard tortoises can reproduce at roughly 10 inches (25.4 cm) SCL. Both sexes will get larger than this, but this is an approximate minimum adult size.

## Sexing

At the breeding size, the sex of the tortoise is very easy to determine. The male is usually smaller than a female of the same age, but the most obvious distinguishing factor is the length of the tail. The male of both tortoise types will have a very long tail as compared to the female. The males will also have a concave plastron. In the leopard tortoise, the male will sometimes be more elongated in shape, while the female is rounder. With the sulcata, the shape differs in that the female is more elongated than the male, but this is not a consistent trait. Tail length is the most reliable indicator of sex.

In adult leopard tortoises, the female is usually larger than the male. The male has a longer tail and a concave rather than flat plastron.

## Breeding Cues

If your tortoises are housed outdoors, breeding behavior can be triggered by the onset of rain, a change in barometric pressure, or a sudden change in temperature. These are some of the cues that seem to trigger this type of behavior. Some other cues that are suspected to trigger breeding behavior are a lack of food availability, drought followed by rain, or cool weather followed by warm weather. In many cases, if you separate the sexes for a time and then reintroduce them there is usually an increase in activity, which also sometimes leads to breeding activity. Seasonal cycles seem to have an influence on the breeding cycles of these tortoises, but not as much as in those species that come from more temperate climatic zones.

## Courtship and Mating

For many tortoises the mating ritual can be quite violent, sometimes to the point that the female is either killed or severely injured. This is not the case with the leopard tortoise, but can sometimes be the case with sulcatas. It is for this reason that when any breeding behavior is noted with the sulcata, it is a good idea to observe the tortoises to be sure the female is not harmed.

Leopard tortoises tend to be less confrontational than most other tortoises; unlike other species, the male does not usually ram the female but instead circles the female to try and get her to stand still by biting at her feet. This is more the rule than the exception, but there are individuals that can get aggressive. This behavior is usually a precursor to breeding.

Male sulcatas, on the other hand, can be quite aggressive in their pursuit of the female. As the size of the tortoise increases, the damage a male sulcata can inflict on a female can be severe. Male sulcatas can be quite territorial. This requires

Male sulcata pursuing a female. Seasonal and weather changes can stimulate breeding activity.

careful consideration when stepping into the enclosure of a 200-pound (90.7-kg) male sulcata. The sulcata is well known for ramming, and a tortoise of that size can inflict severe pain to both another tortoise and the unsuspecting keeper as well.

Breeding can get intense between the tortoises. Occasionally, one tortoise is flipped over by another. If the one tortoise cannot right itself, it can die if is trapped under a heat source or is in a source of water. Take care to reduce the chance of this situation by providing visual barriers in the enclosure and a substrate or structure that the tortoise can obtain a grip on so that it can right itself.

Once breeding behavior starts, you eventually will see the male mount the female from the rear with

## Clutch Size Versus Egg Size

**Sulcatas and leopards can deposit anywhere from 5 to 20 or more eggs, depending on the size of the adults. The number of eggs is also dependent on the size of the eggs. Large adults have been known to deposit both large numbers of small eggs and small numbers of large eggs.**

his front legs on the top of the female's shell and his neck outstretched so that his head is above the female's head. The male will often open its mouth and let out a grunt that can be quite loud in the case of the sulcata but less so in the leopard tortoise. The point is that these tortoises can be very vocal during the actual mating process.

In the wild as well as in captivity, mating usually takes place in the spring through the early summer and can occur almost on a daily basis. Note that breeding does not necessarily indicate that you are going to get fertile eggs. The female first has to be ovulating at the time, and the male has to be not only successful in copulating but also must be successful at delivering the

Sulcatas mating.

Mating pair of leopard tortoises. Note how much larger the female is than the male.

sperm. Because the means in which tortoises mate is so primitive, the chances of fertilizing the eggs on a single mating is not very good. This is why it is very difficult if not impossible to predict when you can expect eggs after mating. It is commonly understood among tortoise breeders that the greater the frequency in the occurrences of mating, the greater are the chances of obtaining fertile eggs.

## Egg Laying

After mating has occurred, you can possibly get fertile eggs at any time from one to five years. Tortoises have been known to retain sperm for that long. In the wild, females normally deposit eggs in the fall or in the spring. In most areas where these tortoises are kept as pets, they can deposit eggs at any time of the year with no real pattern, although once they do start depositing eggs in a particular climate they usually develop a pattern that remains fairly consistent. Leopard tortoises can lay eggs up to eight months out of the year at roughly 30-day intervals. Sulcatas can be just as consistent and productive.

## Nesting

If the female is carrying fertile eggs, right before she is ready to lay them she will display a restless behavior that appears to be a quest. She will pace the perimeter of the enclosure more so than usual. She will walk, sniff the ground, walk some more, and sniff the ground again. This ritual can continue until she finds a nesting site that meets her liking. Why the the female chooses a particular nesting site is not really known, but many times once a nesting site is chosen the same tortoise will choose the same general area nest after nest.

Although you might see the tortoise pacing, you might not actually see her nesting. This can present a major problem, because if you don't see the tortoise nesting you will most likely not know that she has nested. These tortoises are very good at hiding and covering up nesting sites. Most of the time nesting will occur in the afternoon, but this is not a hard and fast rule. It does, however, give you a possible time reference as to when to be on the alert for the tortoise to nest.

If you do not actually see the tortoise deposit the eggs, it is almost impossible to find the nest. After laying the eggs the tortoise will cover the eggs and pack the earth down on top of them. She will then scrape the ground that has covered the nest and move surrounding debris over it. Many times she will also move away from the nest and scrape the ground in an area some distance from the actual nest. This gives the appearance of another nest. When the tortoise is finished with the entire process the nest totally blends in with the surrounding area.

The sulcata is unique in that the female usually nests on the front berm of its burrow. This is the mound of dirt that is piled up in front of its tunnel entrance. The female will first dig a large hole that it can actually fit its whole body into. It will then dig a

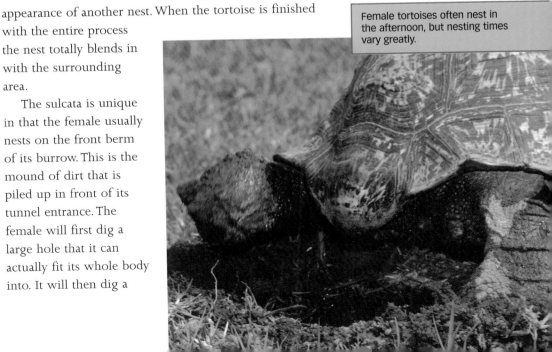

Female tortoises often nest in the afternoon, but nesting times vary greatly.

typical flask-shaped nest in that hole, similar to the hole used by most other tortoises.

## Retrieving the Eggs

If the tortoise is caught nesting you will have the choice of allowing her to finish nesting or collecting the eggs as they are dropped. Collecting the eggs is recommended, since the eggs are sometimes cracked as they are dropped into the nest.

If collecting the eggs as they are dropped is not possible, the eggs can be collected as soon as there is an indication that nesting is complete. This is usually signaled by the tortoise's starting to cover the eggs. At this point she can be gently moved after having deposited the eggs. The tortoise will usually display the odd behavior of continuing the nesting action regardless of where you move her. The eggs can then be removed after the tortoise is moved. Once the eggs are removed she is gently placed back over the nest and allowed to complete the nesting process.

Both sulcatas and leopards lay between 5 and 20 eggs in a clutch, depending on the size, age, and health of the female.

You can also choose to allow the tortoise to complete the nest and then dig up the eggs later, after the tortoise has moved on. The digging up of the eggs must be approached with extreme care. The soil is usually wet and packed down very hard. As a result of this it is very easy to damage the eggs while trying to remove the substrate from around the eggs in the nest. It is also recommended that tools not be used to remove the substrate from the nest for the same reason. Once you find the nest it is a good idea to dig around the nest and approach the eggs from the side. This will allow the earth to fall away from the eggs as you approach them, which in turn decreases the chances of cracking an egg. When removing the eggs from the nest, you should try to keep the eggs in the same relative position in which they were found; that is, the side of the egg facing up should remain the side of the egg facing up. This is not a crucial point if you remove the eggs as soon as they were deposited, but it becomes more important if the eggs were allowed to develop for any length of time. Once the embryo begins to develop and increase in size there is a chance that any movement in the egg can damage the connection between the embryo and the yolk. This is true until the embryo is large enough to stabilize itself against the shell. It is always good practice to mark the top of the eggs with a soft-leaded pencil. It is also good practice to record the number of eggs laid in addition to the date and time the eggs were deposited, along with any other information that you might think would be helpful for future reference.

## Egg Retention

If your tortoises are well acclimated, healthy, and active, the nesting process should not be a problem. Occasionally a tortoise will be ready to lay eggs but cannot or will not lay them. Usually these tortoises will eventually either nest or evacuate the eggs without nesting, but as with most other things in biology, there are no certainties.

If you notice a tortoise displaying nesting behavior, it is a good idea to make notes as to the day the nesting behavior began, along with how long the behavior took from start to finish and the location of the nest. The weather conditions are also a good observation to note. Taking these observations down during normal nestings will provide data that can alert you if something is wrong or not normal. These observations can you help you decide whether or not you need to intervene with a tortoise that is not nesting as normal.

# Temperature-Dependent Sex Determination

There is an added dimension to the development of tortoise eggs that is not relevant when breeding snakes, most lizards, or birds. The sex of the developing tortoise is determined by its incubation temperature. This is called temperature-dependent sex determination or TSD. This becomes important when deciding on what temperature you wish to use to incubate the eggs. The most important point to note is that the temperature is going to have to be maintained within a very stable range if you wish to favor one sex or another. At about 86°F (30°C), the sex ratio of the hatchling will be roughly even.

## Be Prepared

If eggs are expected, it is always best to have your egg container already set up. It is also a good idea to have an incubator set up and tested. When the eggs do show up, you will be well prepared, and there will be no emergency to scramble for the necessary equipment. The incubating material can be placed in the egg box and not moistened until the eggs arrive.

Once nesting behavior begins, tortoises generally nest in a day or two. If a week passes and the nesting behavior continues without actual nesting, the tortoise should be watched closely. If the behavior continues beyond a week without any noticeable distress in the tortoise, continue monitoring her. However, take the tortoise to a veterinarian as soon as possible if there are any signs she is in distress, such as a lack of appetite, lethargy, or difficulty in walking. With an X-ray, the vet can determine whether the tortoise is carrying eggs and whether it is necessary to intervene. Many times the tortoise can carry the eggs to the next season and evacuate them then. Should the veterinarian determine that the eggs need to come out, there are drugs such as oxytocin that have been successfully used for inducing laying in turtles. There are more drastic measures, such as surgery, that can be taken if everything else fails, but it rarely comes to that. This is all mentioned as a caution as to what to look for if the normal process does not take place. This does not happen often, and your next concern will normally be what to do with the eggs.

## Incubation

The first option for incubating the eggs is to allow them to remain in the ground where they are deposited to incubate naturally. Your location will determine whether you will be able to allow the eggs to incubate this way. If your climate is as warm or is warmer than the climate of the tortoise's natural habitat, it is possible that the eggs can develop normally. Because of the lack of control and the risks presented by the elements and egg predators, such as raccoons and insects, natural incubation is usually not recommended.

## Egg Structure

The tortoise egg is hard shelled, with a thin inner skin that surrounds the contents and eventually the developing tortoise. The shell is made up of microscopic plates that allow the transfer of air and moisture between the inside and outside of the egg. It is for this reason that the egg needs to be incubated in a relatively humid environment or the egg contents will eventually dry out. Although the egg needs a humid environment, you must be careful not to let the incubation medium get too moist or the exchange of gas is hindered. There is also the added risk of the egg's absorbing too much moisture and cracking. This is a common problem with both sulcata and leopard tortoise eggs. It is for this reason that it is always better to incubate the eggs slightly drier than for many other species.

When eggs are laid they are a translucent white to light yellow color. When they are exposed to the air after being laid they tend to become a more pure white color if they are fertile. The process starts as a spot on top of the egg and migrates down and around the egg. This process is what is known as 'chalking' and is usually an indication the egg is fertile, but it  by no means guarantees hatching.

While you can let the eggs incubate in the ground, most breeders excavate them and incubate them artificially.

The time it takes a clutch to hatch is very variable—anywhere from 90 to 400 days for the leopard tortoise.

## The Incubator

Because leopard tortoises and sulcatas are usually maintained outside their natural range, natural incubation is often not practical. It is for this reason that it is usually advisable to collect the eggs and place them in an incubator. Many keepers choose to build their own incubator, which actually adds to the fun and experience of tortoise keeping. A simple incubator consists of a basic insulated box. Add to this a heat source and a means of controlling that heat source in the form of a thermostat. Those are the only necessities. Other items that are added—such as bottles of water and stones to stabilize temperature and dishes of water to maintain humidity—are only added to help in maintaining a stable environment. While these items are not necessary, they do make the process easier.

For the box you can use any container such as a fish tank, plastic box, Styrofoam cooler, or a custom-constructed enclosure. For the heat source, a standard bulb in a ceramic fixture or a ceramic emitter can be used. The last major consideration is going to be the temperature control, which can be accomplished by a wafer switch or some other form of thermostat. There are other ways to set up the incubator, but these suggestions are probably the most cost effective. There are also commercial incubators that can be purchased ready to go.

All of the items listed so far should already be in place if there is any indication that your tortoise is going to lay eggs. It is always a good idea to have the incubator set up and ready to go long before the eggs actually arrive. If the eggs do show up unexpectedly, you can place them in a container with the incubation medium and then place that in an area that maintains a relatively stable temperature, such as a boiler room or on top of a hot water heater, until you can get the incubator constructed.

## Setting Up the Eggs

The eggs should be placed in a container with a substrate (often called the incubation medium) that will hold moisture. Many keepers use sand, vermiculite, perlite, or a mixture of these items. Another substrate that has arrived on the market that has some good properties for this application is ground coconut shell or husk. It retains the moisture the eggs need but can be kept drier so the eggs can breathe.

Standard practice when setting up the incubation medium is to moisten the substrate in a ratio of one part water to two parts substrate, by weight, to start with. Remember the consistency of the substrate at this ratio because as the substrate dries out you want to maintain the same consistency or just a little drier.

The eggs are then placed within the incubation medium, buried half way or less. Space the eggs roughly one-half inch (1.3 cm) apart so that if any of the eggs go bad they will not have an effect on the good eggs. The egg container should have some holes 1/8 to 1/4 inch in size to allow for air exchange, but you don't want so many that the substrate dries out too quickly. The container should then be covered.

Inspect the eggs every week or so for any eggs that have gone bad and to check the moisture level of the substrate. If the eggs are fertile, they will begin to chalk after a day or two but will sometimes show signs of chalking a few hours or even many days after they have been laid.

## Incubation Temperature

The temperature at which the eggs are incubated is very important. Temperatures that are too warm or too cold will harm or kill the embryos. Incubation temperature has an additional importance in turtle: the sex of the tortoise is dependent on the temperature at which the egg is incubated; there are no sex chromosomes, as there are in mammals. This is called temperature-dependent

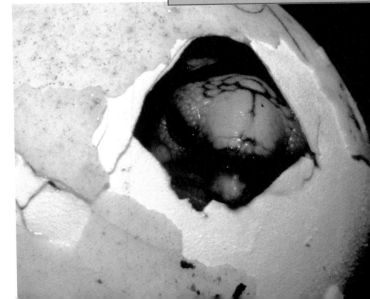

Once a hatching tortoise pips the egg, it may sit in there for some time before completely emerging.

sex determination. It is found in all known turtles, crocodilians, and some lizards.

A few studies have been done on this topic, but the information that has been attained so far has shown that there is a single temperature at which there is an even number of males and females that develop in a clutch of eggs. Below that temperature one sex is favored and above that temperature the other sex is favored. This sounds simple enough, but there is much that is not known. For example, in some species of reptiles there is a second and even a third temperature at which the ratios change to favor one sex or the other. Currently the assumption for tortoises is that below a certain temperature you get all of one sex and above that temperature you get all of another, but more research may modify this.

It is becoming clearer that 86°F (30°C) is a common crossover temperature for many chelonians, and it is the case with sulcatas and leopard tortoises. Above this temperature, you can expect the hatchlings to be predominantly females and below that you can expect mostly males. Just keep in mind that in biology there is only one certainty: that there are no certainties. Many keepers allow the incubator temperature to vary plus or minus 2°F (1.1°C) to increase the chances of a good mix of male and female hatchlings.

Temperature also has an effect on the rate at which the egg develops. With a decrease in temperature, there is a corresponding decrease in developmental rate, and the tortoise takes longer to reach hatching size. With an increase in temperature, there is also an increase in the rate at which the tortoise develops. If the temperature is too high, there is a corresponding increase in physical deformities that can be something as minor as extra scutes to as drastic as missing limbs or even added limbs. Clearly, it is important to control incubation temperature.

## Incubation Duration

The duration of incubation is highly variable among both of these tortoises, even with a constant temperature. The incubation can be as short as 90 days to as long as over 400 days in the case of the leopard tortoise. What is interesting to note is that once an incubation period has been established for a particular female, it seems to remain consistent. For example, a tortoise that has a clutch that hatches in 100 to 130 days can be expected to have this hatch rate with subsequent clutches. One hundred to 150 days is a normal average range you can expect for both the sulcata and the leopard tortoise.

After about 90 days, check the incubator on a daily basis. It is not critical if you miss a day once in a while, because a hatchling tortoise can survive for well over a month without food after hatching as long as it is in an environment in which dehydration is kept to a minimum. This will be the case if the incubation medium is kept moist.

## Hatching

Prior to the egg hatching, there is usually a noticeable discoloration of the egg. This is due to the baby tortoise's scratching and tearing the inner membrane that surrounds it in the egg. The discoloration usually occurs where the head is positioned in the egg and is accomplished by the egg tooth or foreclaws tearing the membrane. The egg tooth is a small hornlike projection on the upper mandible just below the nostrils. Its only use is to aid the tortoise in punching a small hole in the egg; this is often called pipping. The egg tooth falls off shortly afterward. When the tortoise pips the egg, it will normally remain in the egg until all the yolk is absorbed into the body. Like an embryonic bird, a tortoise has a large yolk attached to it through an umbilical cord. The yolk serves as a source of nutrients. When the embryo has developed enough to survive outside the egg, the tortoise will draw any remaining yolk into its shell through the umbilical attachment site, which is on the center line of the belly.

Occasionally a tortoise will emerge from the egg before it has had a chance to fully absorb the yolk. This is very common among leopard tortoises. If the yolk sac is ruptured in this instance, it can lead to an infection fairly quickly. To remedy this situation, place the tortoise in a small container with moist paper toweling on the bottom. Place the tortoise on top of the paper. For the container you can use a coffee cup or a small deli container. The type of container you use is not really important as long as the tortoise's movements are restricted so that it does not rupture the yolk sac. Unless the tortoise is severely premature, the yolk will be totally absorbed within a few days.

Occasionally a hatchling will come out of the egg before it completely absorbs the yolk. It will need special care until it does so.

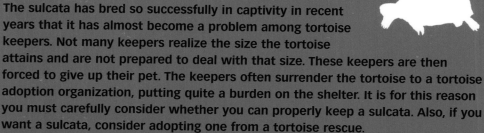
The time in which it takes an egg to hatch is extremely variable. Sometimes the eggs hatch quickly, and sometimes they take quite a long time. This hatch rate also varies from individual to individual; some tortoises lay eggs that hatch out in a short amount of time and some lay eggs that take longer to hatch. The point here is to be patient. If the hatching tortoise is a healthy animal, it will eventually hatch. On the other hand, if the tortoise is weak and feeble it probably would not survive anyway. It is not always a good idea to help a tortoise hatch out; the majority of the time more viable tortoises are harmed than weak tortoises are saved. Allow the eggs to go full term and do not be tempted to open the egg early. If you notice the discoloration that was mentioned earlier, it is probably all right to carefully open the egg. Otherwise it is best to leave the egg alone until you are certain it has gone bad or it hatches.

When the tortoise first hatches it will sometimes look deformed from being folded up in the egg. For the first week the shell remains fairly plastic and will fill out to its normal shape if the humidity is maintained at a high enough level. It is for this reason that the tortoise can be placed in the same setup as the premature tortoise. This will allow the tortoise to easily flatten out and attain its normal shape.

## Oddities and Morphs

Occasionally the genetic packages of a breeding pair of tortoises connect in such a sequence that an offspring that would normally not survive in the wild hatches. In tortoises, the most common trait to fall under this distinction is the albino, but there are some color other color varieties (called morphs) in addition to albinos. Occasionally also, a two-headed tortoise is able to survive, but this is not very common. Some tortoise keepers see these deviations as flaws when compared to the natural animal and suggest that such unfit animals be destroyed to maintain genetic purity, while other tortoise keepers see them as marketable traits.

In the case of the sulcata the color morphs have actually become desirable, and some of them fetch a hefty price. On the other hand, the leopard tortoise can be raised in such a manner (hot and rather humid) that the black pigment is reduced to produce a very light if not-quite- white tortoise. This is usually not a genetic trait but a developmental trait that seems to be unique to leopard tortoises. Even though this does not look very natural, it is quite appealing to many tortoise keepers. The idea here is that these animals are pets and should be treated as such. Even the genetic freaks have their intrinsic beauty, and there will always be someone who will be more than willing to give them a home.

One final point that needs to be mentioned in this section, and that's this: you really cannot look at raising and breeding tortoises as a financial investment. There are many people who use investment as a selling pitch for some tortoises. If you consider the time you take to properly raise your tortoise and the length of time it takes for it to reach maturity, which can normally take upwards of 10 years or more, you will quickly realize that raising tortoises for financial gain is a very poor investment. Many keepers do sometimes amass a collection that can and does make them money, but the time and energy they put into the project could easily make them more in other markets. Those who do make a living out of raising tortoises usually have demonstrated their passion and commitment to the raising of their tortoises and reap the dividends only after a long time and an excessive amount of work. This, of course, does not consider one other very large and important factor—luck. Regardless of how much knowledge you have of a tortoise and its requirements, if you do not have one single pair that is compatible this final stage in the life of your tortoise is sure to fail. This one last factor is ultimately the result of luck. This whole idea is being pointed out because many keepers seem to lose sight of the reason they keep tortoises. It is a rewarding feeling to raise a creature from birth to adulthood and watch the cycle continue. That should be reward enough.

# Chapter 6

# Health Care

The two most important points in the health of your tortoise have been constantly stressed throughout this guide, and they are going to be stressed here again. Heat and hydration together form your greatest insurance against most causes of ill health. This of course assumes that you have a healthy tortoise to begin with and you are feeding it a good healthful diet. These components lay the foundation for a tortoise that should in all likelihood outlive you. However, there are outside influences that you will not be able to control such the heat dropping off in the middle of a cold December night or parasite-carrying birds taking a bath in you tortoise's water dish. These are the kinds of things that seem harmless enough but can be devastating to the health of your tortoise if precautions are not taken.

## Signs of Illness

It is important to know what your tortoise acts like during normal conditions. You should be concerned if your tortoise should suddenly stops eating or becomes less active. Along with being signs of ill health, these behaviors can cause the tortoise's health to move into a downward spiral. If you observe them, look for other indications of sickness, such as eyes are not fully open or the presence of a runny nose. As soon as you notice a sudden change in behavior, watch the tortoise carefully and make certain that it is warm and well hydrated.

Another sign to look for is the appearance or shape of the tortoise's feces. Believe it or not, this is a commonly discussed topic among tortoise keepers—although it is not a very pleasant subject. The feces should be firm and well formed in the shape of a pellet. If the feces are runny and without any shape, there is a good chance there are health issues that should be addressed. This of course also depends on what you have been feeding your tortoise. High-moisture foods such as melons and overripe fruits will also cause runny stools. Some foods, such as beets, will change the color of the feces also.

Tortoises can hide illnesses until they are very sick, so take your pet to a reptile veterinarian as soon as you notice something wrong.

All of the signs of ill health will increase in severity as time goes on if the problem is not detected and corrected. If the tortoise begins to dehydrate because you do not notice it is not taking water, the eyes will start to have a sunken-in, hollow appearance. The discharge from the nose will sometimes increase with time. There will also be a noticeable loss of weight due to the tortoise's not eating. The tortoise will develop a hooked appearance to the forelimbs. This is especially noticeable in debilitated leopard tortoises.

## Parasites

One of the more common health issues among tortoises is

parasites. These can be ectoparasites (parasites that are external to the body), such as ticks, mites, and some worms. The other type of parasites is endoparasites (parasites that live inside the body). These include most worms and protozoans. In all likelihood, you selected a captive-born and -raised tortoise with the assumption that it is free of parasites. However, the ease in which a tortoise can become infected with parasites is amazing. The possibility of a bird that bathes in the water bowl having parasites that it can transmit to your or anyone else's tortoise is relatively high. Any tortoise that is kept outdoors is at risk for picking up parasites. This in itself is not a grave concern, because most tortoises can live with a limited parasite load if they are fit and healthy. If the health should decline for any reason, parasites will reproduce explosively and debilitate or kill the host.

For the most part, a parasite does not want to kill its host, but if the host becomes debilitated for any reason, the parasite can overwhelm the host. The parasite has evolved to survive as long as the host does, and there are checks and balances to make this happen as long as the host is healthy. Once that balance tilts in the favor of the parasite, it usually continues to escalate in favor of the parasite, which leads to other problems. For the tortoise, this can happen if the tortoise contracts some other illness or the parasites are not kept in check by good diet and keeping conditions. This is one of the reasons that fiber is important in a tortoise's diet. It is suspected that the fiber has a cleansing effect on the digestive system of the tortoise. With the ectoparasites, the situation is similar in that the tortoise can coexist with the parasite as long as the tortoise is healthy and the parasites are kept in check by being knocked off as the tortoise burrows and forages.

The parasite load is usually very high in wild-caught tortoises. Remember that as long as there is a balance between the health of the tortoise and the parasite load there should be little impact on the health of the tortoise. The problem arises because the stress of collection is always overwhelming. Add to this overcrowded conditions and exposure to improper temperatures before the tortoise ever makes it to the pet shop, making it likely the parasites are debilitating the host. The more time that passes before the tortoise receives proper care,

Outdoor housing has many benefits, but it exposes your tortoise to the risk of contracting parasites.

the greater the chance that the tortoise will never recover. If you do find yourself in the situation that tempts you to purchase a wild-caught tortoise, always ask how long the tortoise has been in captivity. The shorter the time, the better are the chances of survival for the tortoise. This is one of the main reasons you should select a tortoise born and raised in captivity whenever possible.

## The Shy Leopards

Examining a leopard tortoise for signs of ticks or botflies can be a problem, because leopard tortoises have a tendency to be very shy and withdrawn when picked up. It is for this reason that you must handle the tortoise gently and slowly so as to gain its trust. Try to get the tortoise to trust you enough to allow you to touch its head without withdrawing. Over time, most tortoises will stop withdrawing, which will make examination and giving medication that much easier. This can take anywhere from a few weeks to never. It all depends on the personality of the individual tortoise, because some tortoises are more shy than others and some are more adaptable to captivity than others.

## Ectoparasites

Ectoparasites are a minor problem for the most part. They can be removed physically by a brush in the case of mites or by careful removal using tweezers in the case of ticks. The tick can be removed by grasping the tick and, with a steady force, pulling it backward and parallel to the skin. Make every effort to remove the head that is under the skin, but if the head should break off, it should be left alone and the area where the head of the tick remains on the animal should be cleansed with an antiseptic. It is also important that the area in which the tortoise is kept be thoroughly cleaned as well. If you are dealing with an outdoor enclosure this is not realistically possible, apart from the general cleanup of removing animal waste and leftover food by raking or sweeping up the material. You should continue to monitor the tortoise for any recurrence and remove any parasites that should appear. It will take time, but the parasites will eventually be eradicated. The use of insecticides is not recommended.

One other ectoparasite that shows up occasionally in tortoises but not very often is maggots. These are the larval stage of botflies and become a problem only if a fly is allowed to deposit eggs on some decaying flesh or open wound. From this description you might wonder how this can happen. The tortoise's body has some deep covered pockets that allow some parts of the body to be hidden by the shell. If such a problem is going to develop it will be in the hidden areas, which is why this particular parasite is mentioned. It is always a good idea to give your tortoise an external once-over every time you pick it up.

Wild baby leopard tortoise and a tick pulled off it. Ticks are often found on wild-caught tortoises.

While examining a tortoise, you should pay particular attention to the places where the skin attaches to the shell. Pay particular attention to the areas in the rear of the shell around the legs and the tail. On occasion you should carefully push the tail up and out of the way so you can inspect the area where skin attaches to the shell under the tail.

# White Mites

**Sometimes you might also find some tiny—smaller than a pinhead—white mites present in the substrate. These mites occur if you are using an organic substrate and it is excessively moist. Areas that support these mites can be found around the water bowl or in the area of the humid hide. These particular mites are more of an esthetic nuisance than any real threat to the tortoise. Cleaning the area and either replacing the substrate or keeping it dry usually eliminates the little pests.**

This is a problem area, so remember to check it. Remember that these parasites are normally not a major concern, because they are rarely if ever present on clean, healthy animals.

## Endoparasites

Endoparasites are the parasites you are most likely to encounter in your tortoise. If the tortoise is an indoor tortoise and it comes from good captive-bred stock, this risk is highly reduced or even eliminated with good health practices. The most obvious indication that something is wrong is if the tortoise has changed its behavior and all environmental conditions have remained unchanged.

If any of the signs mentioned for ill health do show up, the next course of action is to seek veterinary care, because endoparasites are most likely the cause. Be sure to take a fresh fecal sample to the vet with the tortoise. This will allow the vet to look at the sample under a microscope to confirm or eliminate the

Leopard tortoise with a runny nose. A runny nose is usually a sign of a respiratory infection but can have other causes.

possibility of parasites. If you cannot get to the vet, that day you can refrigerate the sample or keep the sample in a cool place where it will keep for a few days. Do not freeze the sample. This will make a good diagnosis more difficult if not impossible.

**Protozoans** The Protozoa comprise a large group of single-celled organisms; the ones that are the most commonly seen in tortoises are the flagellates and amoebas. These are the parasites that are most easily transmitted and are the ones you are most likely to encounter even with captive-born and -raised tortoises.

If protozoans are detected early enough they can be easily eradicated or reduced in number with the proper drugs. The most commonly used drug in the elimination of flagellates and amoebas is metronidazole. This is a very safe and effective drug if used properly. Tortoises seem to have a high tolerance for metronidazole, so even the smallest tortoise can be safely medicated. The dosage for this drug is highly variable, based on the application in which it is used. On the discovery of protozoans through fecal examination, some veterinarians will dose the tortoise using a high dosage over a wide interval. Other applications include dosing the tortoise using lower dosages over shorter intervals. This usually depends on the health of the tortoise and the type of protozoan that is found. It is for this reason that a veterinarian's diagnosis should always be sought even though metronidazole is a readily available drug.

The leopard tortoise seems to easily fall prey to a protozoan called *Hexamita*. These parasites attack the kidneys and are diagnosed through microscopic examination of the urine. Another protozoan that is suspected of infecting the leopard tortoise is the protozoan *Entamoeba*. Even though this organism has not been detected in fecal exams, it is thought of being responsible for causing a slow wasting away of the tortoise. It was once thought that *Entamoeba* was a harmless intestinal dweller, but there is mounting evidence that this might not be the case.

**Parasites Happen**

Tortoises kept outdoors will eventually pick up internal parasites. That is almost a certainty. The sources of transmission are virtually impossible to control, because tortoises can pick up endoparasites via the ground, water, air, insects, and other animals. These parasites frequently cause no problems if you maintain the tortoise in good health and under good conditions.

The parasite migrates out of the digestive tract, embedding itself in other body tissue, and therefore will not always be found in the feces. Treatment is with metronidazole over a lengthy period of time, or with one of the newer drugs that kill the parasite in any stage of its development.

**Worms** Parasitic worms, or helminths, include the flatworms, tapeworms, and roundworms. Roundworms are the ones most commonly seen in tortoises, although the others show up on occasion. The diagnosis for the helminths is very similar to that of the protozoans. A fecal sample from the tortoise is examined under a microscope to look for the eggs or the organism itself. Occasionally the tortoise will pass a worm in its stool, and the worm can be quite large in relation to the size of the tortoise.

For the helminths the drug of choice is usually fenbendazole, but it all depends on what species of helminths are found. The dosage will also vary according to the course of action a particular veterinarian chooses to use. Fenbendazole is another safe drug, but there has been some recent evidence that suggests that some animals react adversely to it if it is used at high dosages over a long period of time. Currently this has not been well documented in tortoises, but it is something keepers should be aware of.

**Other Endoparasites** While other endoparasites that infest tortoises, such as blood parasites, are not commonly encountered in captive-bred tortoises, they can be quite common in wild-caught tortoises. Not a great deal is known about these parasites in tortoises because they are very difficult and expensive to properly diagnose. Historically, they are usually found on necropsy (detailed examination of a dead tortoise). For this reason it is not known whether these parasites are actually pathogenic or not. Parasites in general are frequently seen in tortoises but, as stated earlier, they do not always cause problems. Any problem with both internal and external parasites can be greatly reduced or even eliminated with good husbandry practices.

# Infections

Bacterial and viral infections are another health issue commonly seen in tortoises, but very little is actually known about the effects of many of these bacteria and viruses on tortoises. Some of the above-mentioned symptoms can be attributed to these organisms.

Bacteria are implicated in colds, pneumonia, and infected injuries. Some common bacteria are easily identified in cultures and as a result are easily diagnosed and easy to prescribe for. Most veterinarians will choose to use a broad-spectrum antibiotic rather than to actually culture out a bacteria, because so little is actually known about the effects many bacteria have on tortoises.

## Respiratory Infections

One common health issue that is most likely caused by bacteria is respiratory infection. This usually occurs when the tortoise is stressed and the environmental conditions are suboptimal for that species. The leopard is especially susceptible to respiratory disease at low temperatures. Runny discharge from the nostrils is one of the first signs of respiratory distress, but it differs from the usual runny nose in that the discharge is usually very thick and mucosal. This will be one to the first signs of respiratory infection, but as the disease progresses it seems to move to the glottis, the opening in the throat that leads to the trachea and eventually to the lungs. The infection can be very difficult to treat if it reaches the lungs.

It is hard to notice labored breathing in a tortoise because of the shell, but if you take notice of normal breathing when the tortoise is healthy, you can see a difference in the pumping action of the head and legs when the tortoise is in respiratory distress. It will become more apparent and you will notice an actual

Visible blood within the layers of the shell is a sign of septicemia, a life-threatening condition.

# Good Husbandry Means Good Health

**Bacterial infections usually result from some kind of deficiency in the care of your tortoise. If you pay close attention to the details of care and how your tortoise responds to that care, bacterial infections can be minimized or even eliminated.**

wheezing or bubbling with each breath. A light tap on the tortoise's nose will sometimes help you to hear this when the tortoise quickly withdraws. If there is congestion in the lungs, it can also be seen with the aid of an X-ray of a profile of the carapace. The lungs lie to the left and right of the centerline, just under the top one-third of the tortoise's shell. The upper surface of the lung is separated from the carapace by only a thin membrane.

If respiratory illness is suspected, make sure the tortoise's ambient temperature is at least 80°F (26.7°C) but not higher than 90°F (32.2°C) if there might be a chance of overheating because of the animal's being in a debilitated state from not being able to regulate its own temperature by moving either to or from a heat source. Also, be certain to soak the tortoise daily.

Sick humans are often advised to keep warm, get plenty of rest, and drink plenty of fluids. This also works with tortoises. This line of thought even goes one step further to the similarities of cold treatment in humans in that veterinarians are now administering citric acid to help fight the infection. Citric acid is a major component in orange juice and reported to strengthen the immune system. These suggestions are your courses of action when you notice something is wrong. It is intended to give you some time to get your tortoise to a veterinarian where it can get a proper diagnosis and care. While antibiotics are relatively easy to find, it is not recommended that you diagnose and treat your tortoise on your own. The best course of action always is to seek out the advice of a veterinarian.

## Other Bacterial Infections

Bacteria are also implicated in many septic infections (also called septicemia) that sometimes show up in tortoises. It is relatively common in tortoises that are less than one year old. Septic infections are infections of the blood, and they can be very difficult to treat. They are usually associated with renal failure, which in turns leads to liver failure. The telltale signs of a septic infection are the appearance of blood between the keratin layer and the bone of the shell. By the time a tortoise shows any signs of septicemia, there are usually the other signs of illness that were previously mentioned. The tortoise should have seen a vet long before you notice these signs. This is mentioned here because if you ever do see these signs in a tortoise that you might be interested in purchasing it is highly recommended that you pass the animal by; if you don't, the odds are very high that it will pass on you.

Open wounds are another source of bacterial infection that needs to be mentioned. Your tortoise could receive an open wound as a result of an aggressive breeding, an accident, or, most commonly, the result of an attack by another animal, such as a dog, cat, or a raccoon or any other wild animal. In the event that your tortoise receives any open wound, you should take it to a vet as soon as possible. For minor cuts, place the cut under running water. Do not wipe the cut. Further cleanse the cut with povidone-iodine. Finally, cover the cut with a good triple antibiotic ointment. Try and keep the tortoise in a clean, warm, and dry environment until the cut scabs over. A container with a towel or newspaper substrate is recommended for this.

## Metabolic Bone Disease

Occasionally, regardless of how careful or diligent you are in maintaining your tortoise, you still will run into health issues that originate from an environmental or dietary shortcoming. By providing a varied diet under good environmental conditions, your chances of this happening are greatly reduced. One of the most common dietary deficiencies encountered among tortoises in general is metabolic bone disease (MBD). This is far less commonly seen now than in the previous years of keeping tortoises, but it does show up more often than it should.

The unique trait of the tortoise is its shell, which is modified and expanded ribs. You can see by the mass of the shell that there is a high percentage of bone. It is mainly for this reason that the calcium requirement of tortoises is so high.

## A Secure Pet

The overzealous actions of the family pet, and more specifically the family dog, are one of the most common causes of traumatic injuries in tortoises. Our common domestic pets are hunters by instinct, and for unknown reasons tortoises seem to be enticing prey to them. If you have a dog or a cat, never leave your tortoise unattended with these pets, no matter how much you trust them. Also, make sure that the tortoise is secure in its enclosure with no possibility for the other family pet to gain access. All it takes is one accident, and the feeling of letting your pet down never goes away.

A proper diet, sunlight, and calcium supplementation should prevent MBD in your tortoise.

## Calcium Metabolism

A simple explanation of calcium metabolism follows to provide insight into this mineral's important role in the body of a tortoise.

The interaction of vitamin D along with the hormones calcitonin and parathyroid hormone maintain the level of calcium in the blood within an optimal range. The precursor for vitamin D is obtained from plant material. When the precursor is digested, it is transported by the blood to the skin. When exposed to UVB, it is then converted to another form and then travels to the liver and kidneys to finally be converted to its active form. Vitamin D increases the concentration of calcium in the blood by stimulating uptake of calcium from the food in the intestine. Parathyroid hormone increases the concentration of calcium in the blood by stimulating the release of calcium from the bone and retention of calcium in the kidney. When there is sufficient calcium in the blood, calcitonin causes the calcium to be deposited in the bones and released from the kidneys.

If the kidney fails, vitamin D synthesis is hindered, and calcium is not replenished and continues to be taken from the bone for other functions. From this oversimplification you can see the importance of calcium in normal bodily functions and you can also see the importance the kidney plays in the process.

## Signs of MBD

By having a basic understanding of calcium metabolism, it is easier to understand the importance of each of the steps involved. The things to look for in a tortoise that has MBD are a soft and/or malformed shell and an inability to use its limbs properly. MBD can be avoided by providing a balanced diet containing a good amount of calcium along with UVB from specialized lamps or natural sunlight. Supplemental vitamin D can be provided in place of UVB. Supplemental calcium can also be provided if it is suspected that the tortoise is not getting sufficient calcium from its diet. MBD can be treated if it is not too severe or there is not some other underlying problem such as kidney failure. The treatment is providing adequate calcium along with either a source of UVB or supplemental vitamin D.

## Grooming

Grooming usually does not come to mind when you are thinking of a tortoise, but you might need to trim your tortoise's nails or beak sometimes. This happens more often with tortoises that are maintained indoors on a nonabrasive surface. It can be controlled somewhat by providing a substrate that will provide some wear on the beak and nails. Some keepers provide an abrasive material by adding flat rocks as furniture and as a feeding surface on which the food is placed. Slate or other type of stone commonly used as

## Mixing Species

Any time you add a tortoise to your group, there is always the risk of introducing parasites or disease. Regardless of whether the tortoises are the same species or not, the risk exists. The risk also further increases if you consider keeping different species in the same enclosure. This practice is not recommended without very careful preparation beforehand. The mixing of different species of tortoises out of the wild carries an extremely high risk to the health of all the tortoises in the group because of the introduction of different pathogens that each tortoise might be carrying that the others do not have a tolerance for. This can cause very big problems, and again, is definitely recommended against if any of the tortoises are wild caught or if the keeper does not plan extremely carefully.

Monitor your tortoise's nails and beak to make sure they do not become overgrown.

flagstones is will do for this purpose.

If you closely monitor the length of the beak and nails, you can avoid major complications by trimming these items on regular basis. If you allow the lengths to get too long, the nails and beak becomes more difficult to trim. When it does become necessary to do any trimming it is always easier if your tortoise is used to handling and used to the tools you are going to use. You can condition your tortoise by first handling it on a regular basis to gain its trust.

For both the nails and the beak, you can use an emery board or nail file for light sanding. Because the keratin is laid down in layers it is always easier to sand or file in the direction that the nail is growing and parallel to the surface. Most tortoises will allow you to do this if done in a non-threatening manner, but it does take a little time to gain their trust.

For more drastic trimming, a rotary file is recommended for the beak. If the growth of the beak does reach the length that would necessitate the use of a rotary file, it is suggested that you get a veterinarian or another person who is experienced in this procedure to demonstrate it for you. This will avoid any risk of injury or trauma to the tortoise. Many vets will choose not do this procedure without anesthetizing the tortoise if the overgrowth is too extensive, so it is a good idea to practice a little preventive maintenance so this operation can be avoided.

For the nails, you can use bird nail clippers or dog nail clippers available at most pet shops. It is important to know how far back to clip the nail to avoid cutting the quick. By holding the foot of your tortoise up to the light, you can usually see were the vein ends. You don't want to cut below that point. If you should cut into the vein and cause some bleeding, any styptic pencil or powder will stop the bleeding and reduce any chance of infection. You can use cornstarch if you don't have a styptic pencil handy.

## Temperature Issues

The sulcata and the leopard tortoise do not truly hibernate, although some southern forms of the leopard tortoise do have a kind of winter rest period that some might call hibernation. Both the leopard tortoise and sulcata will also estivate during extremely hot

# The Importance of Hygiene

Washing your hands before and after handling your tortoise is not only a good practice for the health of your tortoise, it is also beneficial to your own health. Reptiles in general have been implicated in the transmission of some diseases harmful to people, notably salmonellosis. Washing your hands with antibacterial soap and hot water after handling your tortoise and the items from its enclosure usually prevents these infections.

Also follow the practice of hand-washing if you have more than one tortoise in different enclosures and you are working from one enclosure to the next. Hand-washing should be practiced when working between the enclosures. If all your tortoises are kept in only one enclosure, hand-washing is not necessary for working within the enclosure but should still be done before and after working with the tortoises.

temperatures or long periods of drought. When these tortoises are maintained outdoors, they will slow down during cooler and excessively hot temperatures or dry conditions.

If your tortoise should experience freezing temperatures, do not raise the temperature too quickly. Bringing the tortoise into room temperatures is sufficient until the tortoise comes around. When you notice the tortoise moving around, you can then slowly move it into more comfortable temperatures.

## Conclusion

This section has covered most of the more common health issues that you are likely to encounter in the care of the leopard tortoise and sulcata. The key to increasing the chances of recovery in the event of illness or injury is to know the behavior and patterns of your tortoise. Knowing your tortoise's normal behavior and habits will ensure that if something does go wrong you can notice it early. As it has been stressed all along, if you should suspect something is wrong, be sure the tortoise is kept warm and well hydrated until you can take it to a veterinarian. Your best resource for finding a vet is to contact other tortoise keepers in your area through your local turtle and tortoise club or pet shop. Not only can other tortoise keepers help you find a vet, but most also are always willing to talk tortoise and share their own experiences, which is always helpful.

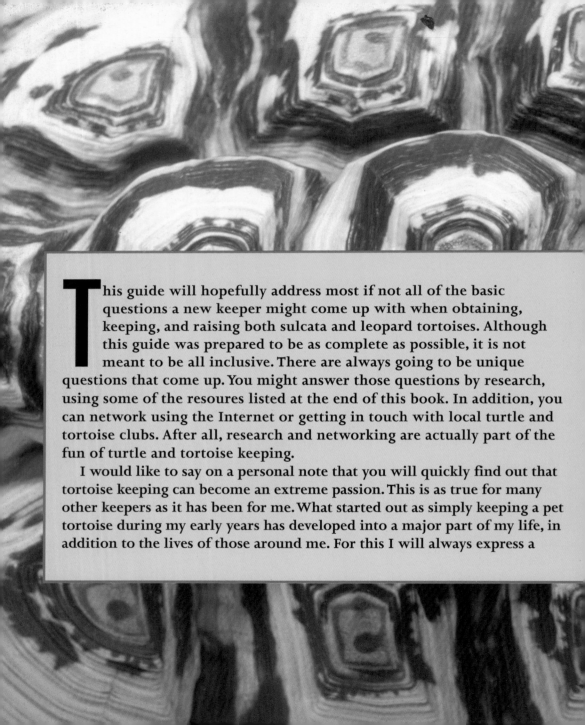

**T**his guide will hopefully address most if not all of the basic questions a new keeper might come up with when obtaining, keeping, and raising both sulcata and leopard tortoises. Although this guide was prepared to be as complete as possible, it is not meant to be all inclusive. There are always going to be unique questions that come up. You might answer those questions by research, using some of the resoures listed at the end of this book. In addition, you can network using the Internet or getting in touch with local turtle and tortoise clubs. After all, research and networking are actually part of the fun of turtle and tortoise keeping.

I would like to say on a personal note that you will quickly find out that tortoise keeping can become an extreme passion. This is as true for many other keepers as it has been for me. What started out as simply keeping a pet tortoise during my early years has developed into a major part of my life, in addition to the lives of those around me. For this I will always express a

# Conclusion

sincere appreciation to my wife of 27 years, Kathy, who had no idea of what she was buying into when she decided to marry me (and it's starting to sink in only now). I would also like to express a great big thanks to my two girls, Danielle and Amanda, who now realize that the level to which their dad has taken his interest is not really normal and not every family has to bring in the tortoises during inclement weather. To my family, thank you for putting up with this odd passion and obsession.

I would also like to thank Ron and Mary Huffaker, Jim Pether, John Coakley, and Donald Schultz  in addition to many others for providing invaluable information for this guide.

My conclusion would not be complete without expressing my sincere appreciation and thanks to all those tortoise keepers that I correspond with the world over who also share this passion for keeping and studying these wonderful animals. My appreciation extends to all chelonian keepers as well as these wonderful creatures.

## Conservation Groups

**The Tortoise Trust**
BM Tortoise
London
WC1N 3XX
UK
http://www.tortoisetrust.org/

**Turtle Conservation Fund**
www.turtleconservation.org/

**Turtle Survival Alliance**
1989 Colonial Parkway
Fort Worth, Texas 76110
www.turtlesurvival.org/

**World Chelonian Trust**
P.O. Box 1445
Vacaville, CA 95696
www.chelonia.org/

## Clubs and Societies

**British Chelonia Group**
P.O.Box 1176
Chippenham Wilts
SN15 1XB
UK
www.britishcheloniagroup.org.uk/

**California Turtle & Tortoise Club**
P.O. Box 7300
Van Nuys, CA 91409-7300
www.tortoise.org

**The Chicago Turtle Club**
6125 N. Fairfield Ave.
Chicago, IL 60659
E-mail: chicagoturtle@geocities.com
www.geocities.com/Heartland/Village/7666/

**German Chelonia Group**
Im Bongert 11a
D-52428 Jülich
www.dght.de/ag/schildkroeten/english/
eschildkroeten.htm

**Mid-Atlantic Turtle & Tortoise Society**
P.O. Box 23686
Baltimore, MD   21203-
E-mail: matts@matts-turtles.org
www.matts-turtles.org/

**New York Turtle and Tortoise Society**
NYTTS
P.O. Box 878
Orange, NJ 07051-0878
E-mail: QandA@nytts.org
nytts.org/

**Society for the Study of Amphibians and Reptiles (SSAR)**
Marion Preest, Secretary
The Claremont Colleges
925 N. Mills Ave.
Claremont, CA 91711
Telephone: 909-607-8014
E-mail: mpreest@jsd.claremont.edu
www.ssarherps.org

## Rescue and Adoption Services

**American Tortoise Rescue**
23852 Pacific Coast Highway, Suite 928
Malibu, CA 90265
Phone: 800-938-3553
Fax: 310-479-4114
Email: info@tortoise.com
http://www.tortoise.com/

**Mid-Atlantic Turtle & Tortoise Society**
P.O. Box 23686
Baltimore, MD 21203
E-mail: matts@matts-turtles.org
www.matts-turtles.org/

**New England Amphibian and Reptile Rescue**
www.ReptileRescue.ne

**PetFinder.com**
www.petfinder.com

**The Turtle Center**
www.turtlecenter.org/

**Turtle Homes**
www.turtlehomes.org

## Veterinary Resources

**Association of Reptile and Amphibian Veterinarians (ARAV)**
P.O. Box 605
Chester Heights, PA 19017
Phone: 610-358-9530
Fax: 610-892-4813
E-mail: ARAVETS@aol.com
www.arav.org

## Websites

**Chelonian Research Foundation**
www.chelonian.org

**Kingsnake.com**
www.kingsnake.com

**Leopardtortoise.com**
www.leopardtortoise.com

**Melissa Kaplan's Herp Care Collection**
www.anapsid.org

**The Sulcata and Leopard Tortoise**
www.africantortoise.com

**Yahoo email groups**
www.groups.yahoo.com

Bonin, Franck, Bernard Devaux and Alain Dupre. 2006. *Turtles of the World*. Baltimore: Johns Hopkins University Press.

Boycott, Richard C. and Ortwin Bourquin. 2000. *The South African Tortoise Book*. South Aftica: Bourquin.

Branch, Bill. 1988. *Field Guide to the Snakes and Other Reptiles of Southern Africa*. Florida: Ralph Curtis Books.

Devaux, Bernard. 2000. *La Tortue Qui Pleure: The Crying Tortoise*. France: SOPTOM

Ernst, Carl H. and Roger Barbour. 1989. *Turtles of the World*. Washington D.C.: Smithsonian.

Fife, Richard and Jerry Fife. 2006. *Leopard Tortoises*. Minnesota: TTPG

Geniez, Philippe, Jose Antonio Mateo, Michel Geniez, Jim Pether. 2004. *The Amphibians and Reptiles of the Western Sahara*. Frankfurt: Chimaira.

Gurley, Russ. 2002. *The African Spurred Tortoise*, Geochelone sulcata, *in Captivity*. Minnesota: Taxon Media.

Harles, Marion and Henry Morlock. 1989. *Turtles: Perspectives and Research*. Florida: Krieger.

Lagua, Rosalinda T. and Virginia S. Claudio. 2004. *Nutrition and Diet Therapy Reference Dictionary*. Iowa: Blackwell.

Loveridge, Arthur and Ernest Williams. 1957. *Revision of the African Tortoises and Turtles of the Suborder Cryptodira*. Massachusetts: Cambridge.

McArthur, Stuart, Roger Wilkinson, Jean Meyer, Charles Innis and Steve Hernandez-Divers. 2004. *Medicine and Surgery of Tortoises and Turtles*. United Kingdom: Blackwell.

Patterson, Rod and Anthony Bannister. 1987. *Reptiles of Southern Africa*. Cape Town: Struik.

Rose, Walter. 1962. *The Reptiles and Amphibians of Southern Africa*. Cape Town: Miller.

Vetter, Holger. 2002. Turtles of the World Vol. 1: *Africa, Europe and Western Asia*. Frankfurt: Chimaira.

Vetter, Holger. 2005. *Leopard and African Spurred Tortoise*. Frankfurt: Chimaira.

Note: **Boldfaced** numbers indicate illustrations; an italic *t* indicates tables.

## About the Author:

E. J. Pirog has been keeping a large group of reptiles with a special focus on tortoises for more than 30 years, including leopards and sulcatas. He frequently writes and lectures on turtle-related topics and is the author of *Complete Herp Care: Russian Tortoises*. He lives near Atlanta, GA with his family and a herd of tortoises

## Photo Credits: